ALISON HOLST
SIMON HOLST

really easy
chicken
RECIPES

First published in 1999 by Hyndman Publishing, PO Box 5017, Dunedin

ISBN 1-877168-25-4

TEXT: Simon & Alison Holst

DESIGN: Di Leva Design

PHOTOGRAPHY:
Sal Criscillo, pages 9, 16, 27, 28, 37, 38, 43, 44, 49, & 50

Lindsay Keats, Front Cover, & pages 10, 15, 21, 22, 55, & 56

HOME ECONOMISTS: Simon & Alison Holst

PRINTING: Tablet Colour Print

All rights reserved. No part of this publication may be reproduced, stored in a retrieval system, or transmitted in any form, or by means electronic, photocopying, recording or otherwise, without prior permission of the publisher in writing.

The recipes in this book have been carefully tested by the authors. The publisher and the authors have made every effort to ensure that the instructions are accurate and safe, but they cannot accept liability for any resulting injury or loss or damage to property whether direct or consequential.

Because ovens and microwave ovens vary so much, you should take the cooking times suggested in recipes as guides only. The first time you make a recipe, check it at intervals to make sure it is not cooking faster, or more slowly than expected.

Always follow the detailed instructions given by manufacturers of your appliances and equipment, rather than the more general instructions given in these recipes.

Acknowledgements

We would like to thank the firms who provided us with the following food and products.

ALISON'S CHOICE Dried fruit, nuts, seeds, etc.
BENNICK'S POULTRY FARM, BULLER RD, LEVIN Fresh eggs
EMPIRE FOODSTUFFS Dried herbs and spices
FERNDALE Parmesan cheese
GENOESE FOODS Pesto
UNIFOODS John West seasonings
LUPI Olive oil and Balsamic vinegar
RIGA Tortillas
SUREBRAND Teflon liners
TARARUA Grated cheese and cultured dairy products

Important Information

For best results, use a standard metric (250ml) measuring cup and metric measuring spoons when you use these recipes. We use the following standards: 1 tablespoon holds 15ml and 1 teaspoon holds 5ml.

All the cup and spoon measures in the recipes are level, unless otherwise stated. Sets of measuring cups make it easier to measure ¼ and ½ cup quantities.

Large amounts of butter are given by weight. Butter packs usually have 50 gram or 100 gram markings on them. Small amounts of butter are measured using spoons (one tablespoon of butter weighs about 15 grams).

ABBREVIATIONS USED:

| cm | centimeter | ml | millilitre | tsp | teaspoon |
| °C | Celcius | g | gram | Tbsp | tablespoon |

We used a 720 Watt microwave oven to cook the microwaved foods in this book. Microwave cooking times are given as a guide only. Alter times to suit the wattage of the microwave oven you use.

really easy
chicken
RECIPES

CONTENTS

Roasts with a difference	6
Great ideas for precooked chicken	13
Easy one-pan dinners	16
Ethnic chicken treats	28
Deliciously spicy chicken dishes	35
Inviting barbecues and grills	51
Chicken salads to beat the heat	54
Adding the trimmings — gravy and stuffing	60
Homemade chicken stock	61

about this
book

Chicken is an increasingly popular choice for the main meal of the day for many people! It comes in a variety of user-friendly pieces, cooks quickly, is tender, reasonably priced, and tastes great!

Simon and I are often asked what we are working on at the moment. Everyone who heard we were writing a chicken cookbook was pleased to hear about it, and nearly all added the query, "Will it have plenty of recipes that I can make easily at the end of a busy day?"

The answer is YES – this whole book is ALL about really easy recipes with wide appeal. It includes a wide variety of recipes, some new, and others which have proved very popular over many years. It also contains a large section where the whole main course is cooked in one pot or pan, or served with rice or pasta.

Whether you are cooking for yourself or a family, by choosing recipes from different sections of our book (see page 3) you should find that you can enjoy chicken in quite different styles, several times each week.

Throughout this book, when we feel that a recipe is best made with a particular cut, we have suggested it. Unless specified otherwise, the chicken in the ingredients list has skin on and bone in, eg., "2 thighs" means two chicken thighs, bone-in and skin-on. This is an important distinction, since boneless, skinless pieces require less cooking. When we think that a boneless, skinless cut is best, we have written this in the ingredients list.

Some of our recipes call for "chicken pieces". Use mixed, skin-on, bone-in portions or single cuts, ie., all thighs, drumsticks, etc. (Remember that large pieces such as a whole leg or a breast-and-wing piece will take a little longer to cook than smaller pieces.)

If you want to use a particular recipe but have a chicken cut other than the one we have suggested, feel free to make substitutions, but expect a cooking time which is longer for larger, thicker or bone-in pieces, or shorter for smaller, thinner or boneless ones.

The cooking times given in our recipes are for fresh or thawed chicken. (Frozen chicken requires longer cooking.)

It is important that chicken is thoroughly cooked. To ensure this, as well as cooking for the suggested times, test by piercing to the centre of the thickest part - if juices run clear, not pink or red, the chicken is cooked. This is especially important for chicken on the bone. Don't use the same board, knife or utensils for uncooked chicken and ready-to-eat foods without washing them thoroughly. Remember to wash your hands as well.

Always refrigerate cooked and uncooked chicken promptly. Unwanted bugs can grow fast at room temperature! Store uncooked chicken at the bottom of the refrigerator where it cannot drip on other foods.

choosing
chicken

You can buy chicken in many different forms. Choose what suits your situation best. Boneless, skinless pieces may seem expensive, but are lean and 100% edible, whereas drumsticks may contain 40% (inedible) bone.

Fresh whole chickens – good value for money, particularly when on special or as "twin packs". Easy to cook as a roast, or for quicker cooking and economy (cheaper per kilo than buying parts) cut into 2 legs and 2 breast quarters with a sharp knife.

Frozen whole – usually the most weight for your dollar, but always compare with fresh whole chicken on special.

Mixed free-flow-frozen or fresh portions – very close in price to whole chicken – watch for specials. Packs contain assorted pieces of differing weights, which are a lower price per kg than packs of pieces of one type only – good for everyday family use and to keep in a home freezer.

Fresh whole legs – (thigh and drumstick, joined) roast in 30 minutes – allow 1 per person – attractive appearance, best precooked if barbecuing.

Thighs, fresh and frozen – bone-in thighs are compact and meaty. The meat is darker than breast, and also more juicy – it doesn't dry out if overcooked. Cook by a method which allows fat from skin to run from meat (and be discarded) during cooking. Difficult to bone-out at home. Usually a little cheaper than fresh when frozen. **Fresh boneless, skinless thighs (thigh fillets)** are quickly cooked. The darker, juicier meat is preferred to breast meat by some – much leaner than skin-on thighs.

Drumsticks, fresh and frozen – usually similar in price to thighs – popular, especially with children. Contain a higher proportion of bone to meat but have good visual appeal. The smaller unit size means they thaw fast and cook more quickly than thighs – useful finger food!

Wing pieces (nibbles), fresh and frozen – small units, easily managed by children. Quickly cooked and popular fingerfood. Contain a high proportion of bone to meat – although reasonably priced, the price for weight of meat is high.

Breasts – available skin-on and bone-in, skin-on and bone removed, and skinless-boneless – usually fresh rather than frozen, unless in bulk. Breasts are very versatile – removing skin and bone is very easy and is a cheaper option than buying boneless, skinless breasts. **Skinless, boneless breasts** are low-fat and lower in calories than most other meats. They are very popular but will dry out if overcooked. **NOTE:** We regard one chicken as having two breasts, usually weighing 100–150g each.

"Tenders", tenderloins, or breast fillets – small muscles from under the larger breast muscles. Very tender, no waste, small convenient size, good for grilling, barbecuing, pan cooking, etc.

Stir-fry and minced-chicken meat (usually made from breast meat). May sometimes be bought ready-prepared – usually costs more than whole breasts, but it is easy to remove skin and slice whole breasts at home.

wine glazed
roast chicken

Wine, butter and herbs give an attractive and flavourful glaze to this delicious roast chicken which makes a good centrepiece for a festive meal.

FOR 4-6 SERVINGS:

- 1 chicken, about 1.4–1.8kg
- rind of 1 lemon or orange, optional
- 3 cloves garlic
- 25g butter
- ¼ cup white wine
- 2-4 sprigs fresh tarragon, thyme or other fresh herbs
- ½ tsp salt
- freshly ground black pepper

Heat the oven to 210°C, or 200°C for fan-bake.

Dry the chicken, inside and out. Using a potato peeler, remove all the coloured rind from a lemon or orange, if you like its flavour. Squash two of the unpeeled garlic cloves with the base of a bottle, and put them, the herbs of your choice and the citrus rind, in the body cavity.

Sit a doubled piece of unpunctured aluminium foil (about 30cm long) in a small roasting pan. Place the chicken on the foil in the empty pan, then lift up the sides of the foil to cradle the chicken. (Do not wrap the chicken in foil.)

Warm the butter, wine, herbs and seasonings together with the finely chopped remaining garlic clove, then brush this mixture over the chicken. Pour the remaining liquid around the chicken, in the foil.

Bake for 1¼–1½ hours, basting several times during cooking with the liquid in the foil. The chicken is cooked when the juice from the thickest part of the thigh is clear rather than pink when pierced with a skewer or sharp knife, the joint moves freely when the leg is pushed, and the skin is golden brown. (If the chicken browns too quickly, lower the heat.)

Pour liquid from inside and around chicken into a small frypan. Skim off any excess fat and boil down, if necessary, to ¼–½ cup. Following directions on page 8, disjoint or carve the bird. Spoon some of the pan liquids over each serving.

NOTE: The foil cradle stops the wine from evaporating, the butter from spattering, and prevents the pan from getting dirty.

microwaved "roast" chicken

When you want to cook a whole chicken in a short time, consider microwaving it. Microwaved chicken does not have the crisp coating of an oven-roasted bird, but it can have an attractive colour and good flavour if marinated.

1 fresh or thawed chicken

Marinade:

- 2 Tbsp dark soy sauce
- 2 Tbsp sherry
- 2 Tbsp Worcestershire Sauce
- 1 Tbsp honey
- 1 clove garlic, crushed or chopped

Mix the marinade ingredients in an unpunctured oven bag. If necessary, heat the marinade in the bag to soften and dissolve the honey. Place the chicken in the bag with the marinade. Squeeze the air from the bag, so the marinade surrounds the chicken. Fasten bag with a rubber band. Turn bag occasionally, leaving the chicken in its marinade for at least 15 minutes, but preferably for an hour. (You can refrigerate the bagged chicken in its marinade for up to 24 hours, if desired.)

When you are ready to cook the marinated chicken, loosen the rubber band, leaving a finger-sized hole so steam can escape during cooking. (Leave remaining marinade in bag.)

Microwave on 70% power, allowing 10 minutes per 500g. Turn chicken over carefully several times during cooking. After cooking for the estimated time, leave to stand for 5 minutes, then check to make sure it is cooked. If it is, you should be able to move the leg easily, and the thigh, when pierced, should show clear, not pink juice. If not ready, cook for longer (still at 70% power) until done.

Lift chicken from bag and pour juices into a shallow bowl. Microwave juices on full power until slightly syrupy, then pour over chicken when serving.

VARIATION: Put 1–2kg of chicken pieces in an oven bag with the marinade used above and cook in the same way, allowing 10 minutes per 500g at 70% power. Rearrange pieces and flip bag over once or twice during cooking.

roast lemon chicken

A crisp, golden-skinned roast chicken is one of the most popular dishes you can serve! Since roast chicken is actually very easy, and a whole chicken is good value for money, it is worth cooking often, making small changes for variety.

FOR 4 SERVINGS:

- 1 fresh or thawed chicken, about 1.4–1.8kg
- 1 small or ½ large lemon
- 2 cloves garlic
- 2–3 sprigs of any fresh herb you like, or a mixture, eg. thyme, oreganum, tarragon, etc. (optional)
- 1 tsp melted butter or oil

Heat the oven to 210°C, or 200°C for fan-bake. If you want to make gravy and stuffing, see page 60. Pat the chicken dry, inside and out (removing giblets, etc.).

Make about 8 deep cuts in the lemon, without slicing right through and squeeze out 1–2 tsp of juice and put aside. Bang the unpeeled garlic cloves flat, using the bottom of a bottle. Put the lemon, garlic and herbs of your choice inside the cavity of the chicken.

Place chicken, breast side up on a Teflon liner or baking paper in a roasting pan. Mix reserved lemon juice and melted butter or oil and rub or brush this mixture over the chicken.

Check suggested cooking times on chicken pack or bake for 1¼–1½ hours. The chicken is cooked when the juice from the thickest part of the thigh is clear, not pink, when pierced with a skewer or sharp knife and the joint moves freely when the leg is pushed.

Drain juices from cavity into the roasting pan and lift chicken onto cutting board. Bend legs outwards away from carcass, using tongs and a sharp knife, and cut off at hip joints. Cut each leg in two if desired. Cut wings off carcass at shoulder joints. Cut down centre of breast and separate breast meat from carcass.

Skim fat from pan juices and spoon remaining liquid over each serving if you like.

VARIATIONS: For plain roast chicken, prepare as above without the lemon (or without the lemon and herbs). Sprinkle the buttered (or oiled) surface with your favourite (commercially made) seasoned salt, or with paprika, cumin and garlic salt.

Roast vegetables around chicken. Cut vegetables such as potato, kumara, pumpkin and parsnip into chunky pieces. Pat dry. Turn in a little oil in a plastic bag. Place around chicken 10–15 minutes after chicken starts cooking. Turn vegetables once during cooking.

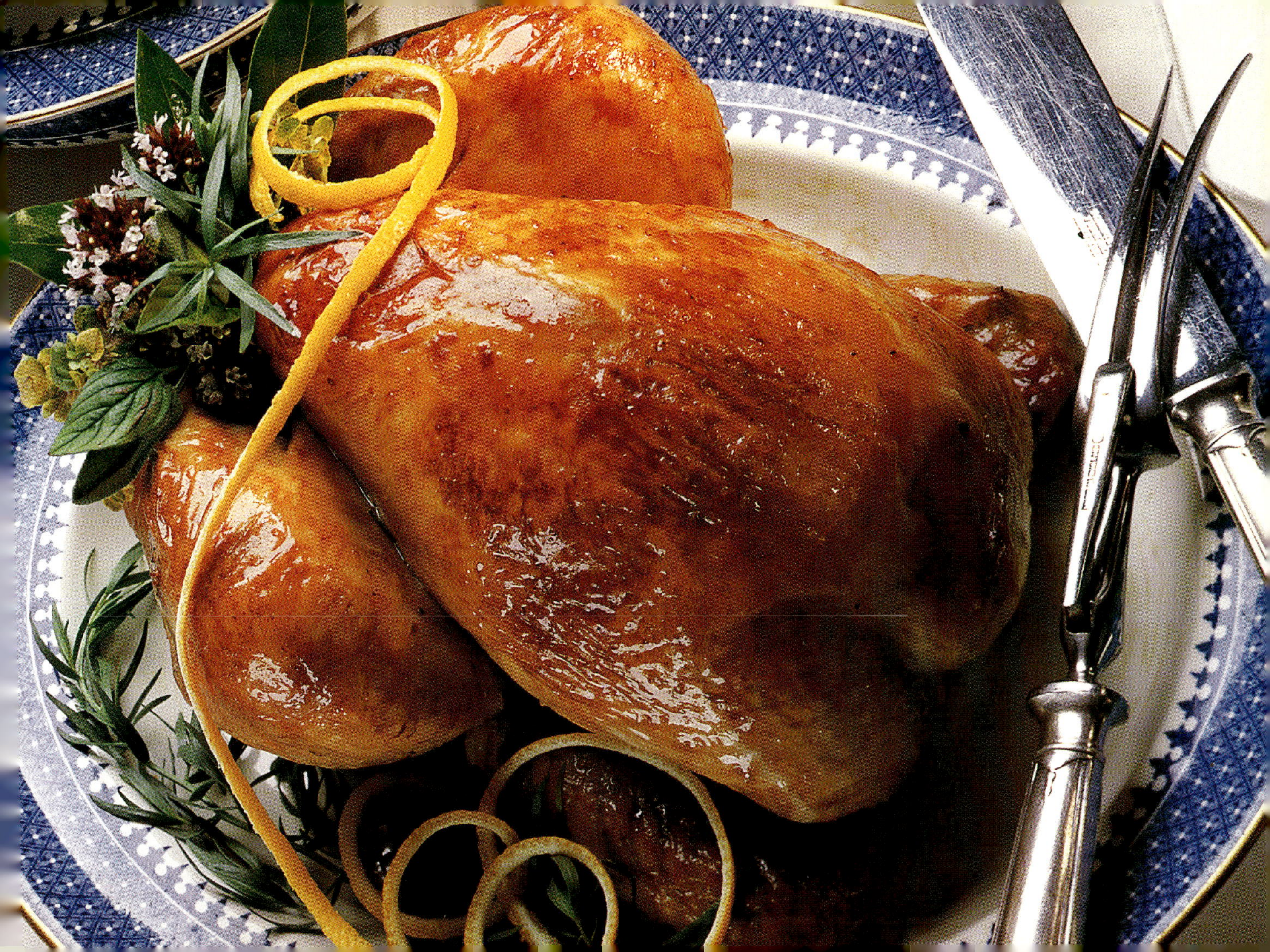

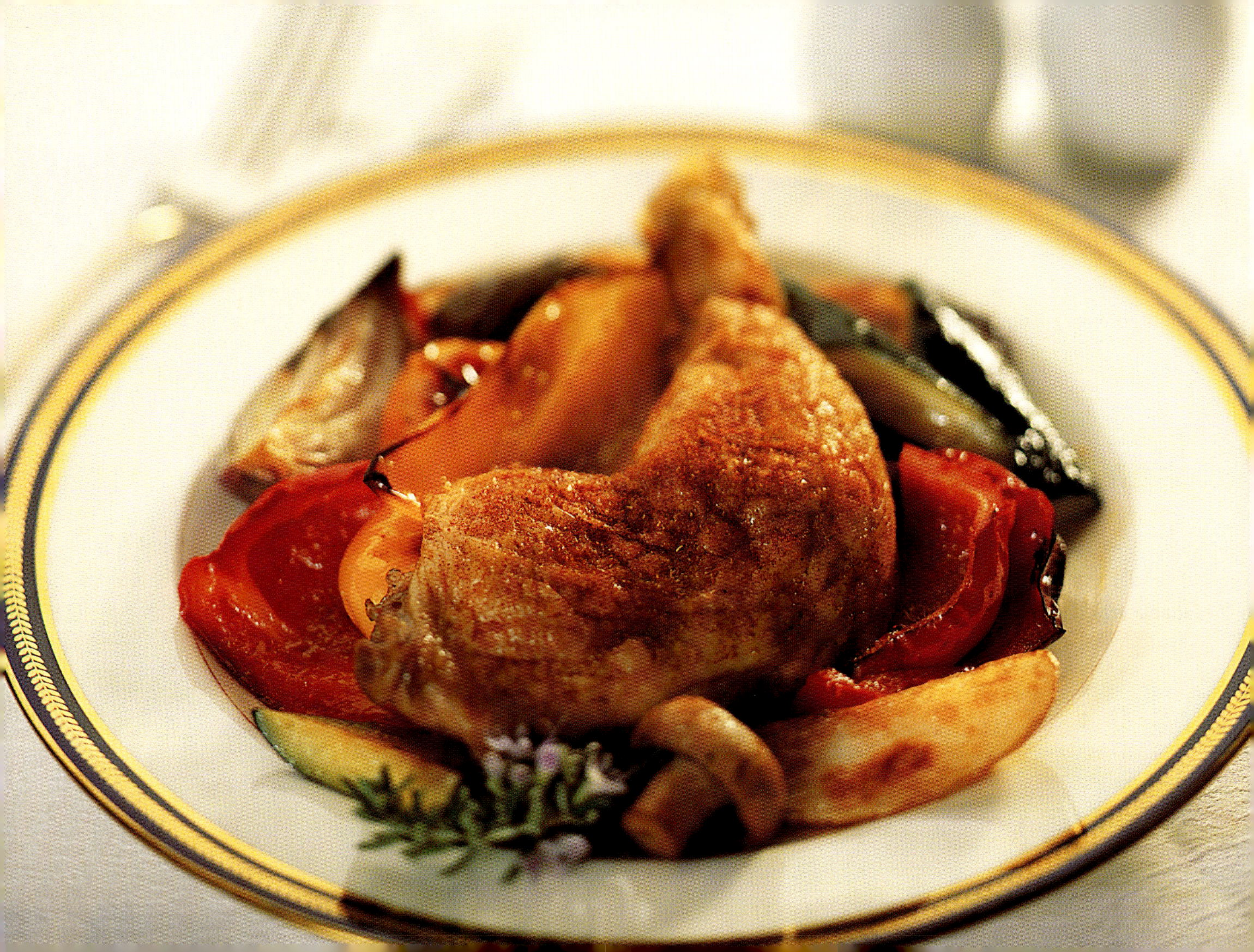

30 minute
roast chicken
and vegetables

A great idea for two people who love roast chicken but who don't have the time or inclination to roast a whole bird. Put everything in the oven and relax while dinner cooks!

FOR 2 SERVINGS:

- fresh rosemary sprigs, if available
- 2 Tbsp olive oil
- 2 crushed cloves garlic
- 2 tsp lemon juice
- 1 tsp ground cumin, optional
- ½ tsp crumbled oreganum, optional
- 2 chicken legs
- enough prepared seasonal vegetables for 2 people (see below)

suitable vegetables include:

- kumara, pumpkin, potatoes and parsnip, peeled and cut into 1cm slices
- red or brown onions
- red, green, yellow, orange peppers
- small eggplant (about 150g), quartered lengthwise
- green and yellow zucchini, halved lengthwise
- whole mushrooms

Heat the oven to 230°C, or 220°C for fan-bake.

Line a roasting pan with a Teflon liner, baking paper or lightly buttered or oiled foil. If you have them, spread fresh rosemary sprigs in the pan. Mix the next 5 ingredients in a large plastic bag. Turn the chicken pieces in this to coat them lightly, then arrange in the pan, and put in the oven to start cooking.

Prepare the vegetables without delay, starting with those needing longest cooking (root vegetables). As each is ready, coat with mixture in bag and place in pan in oven. (Peel and quarter the onion, leaving the root end intact to hold onion together. Quarter peppers and remove the seeds and pith.) Add eggplant, zucchini and mushrooms last, allowing 15–20 minutes cooking time for these.

When chicken has cooked for about 30 minutes, test by piercing with a skewer in the thickest part. It is ready when the juices run clear, not pink. Vegetables should be tender and browned in some places. (Remove them from the pan if cooked before chicken.)

VARIATIONS: Roast the chicken legs without any vegetables in the pan if you like.

Roast Lemon Chicken Legs: Another interesting and flavourful mixture to brush over chicken legs in a lined dish is: ½ tsp grated lemon rind, ¼ cup lemon juice, ¼ cup water or white wine, ¼ tsp dried thyme or tarragon, 2 finely chopped garlic cloves and 2 Tbsp butter. Bake uncovered, at the same temperature for the same time. Cover with foil if legs brown too fast.

NOTE: Any chicken which is to be roasted, may be put in the oven before it is up to heat. Allow a few minutes extra cooking time in this situation.

cheats
"roast" chicken

If you like the idea of chicken with gravy and stuffing, but don't want to be tied to the kitchen by last minute work, try this recipe which can be made ahead and reheated when you want it, without any fuss at all.

FOR 4-6 SERVINGS:

- 1 fresh or thawed chicken, about 1.4–1.8kg
- 1 cup water
- 1–2 rashers bacon
- 1 Tbsp soy sauce, preferably dark
- 2 cloves garlic, finely chopped
- cornflour to thicken
- salt and pepper to taste
- 1 onion, finely chopped
- 2 Tbsp butter
- ½ tsp oreganum
- ½ tsp thyme
- 1–1½ cup fresh breadcrumbs

Place chicken (whole or jointed) in a pot with the water, bacon, soy sauce and garlic. Cover and simmer over a low heat for about an hour, or until flesh is tender. Bone chicken and place chunky pieces of meat in a shallow ovenware dish. Chop the bacon and sprinkle over the chicken. Strain liquid and thicken with a cornflour and cold water paste, until it is gravy consistency. Adjust seasonings to your taste and pour over the chicken.

Cook chopped onion in butter until tender, but not browned. Remove from heat and mix well with the crumbled dried herbs and breadcrumbs. Spread topping evenly over cooled sauce and chicken. Cover and refrigerate until required (overnight if desired).

Reheat, uncovered, at 190°C (or 180°C for fan-bake) for 30–40 minutes or until the topping is crisp and the sauce and chicken are hot.

VARIATIONS: Add chopped sauteed mushrooms to boned chicken and sauce mixture. Serve with boiled new potatoes, or roast potatoes, green beans, or broccoli and carrots.

For a creamier sauce, stir in a few tablespoons of fresh or sour cream.

NOTE: Make fresh breadcrumbs by chopping bread in a food processor, or crumble (or grate) stale crusty bread.

start with a
pre-cooked chicken...

When you've had a really busy day, grab a cooked chicken from your supermarket and dress it up. Use rotisseried, precooked deli, or smoked chicken, in one of the following ways.

Arrange chicken pieces skin side up in a shallow ovenware dish, and pour herb-flavoured packaged gravy mix (thinned to a coating consistency) over them. Or put the pieces on a bed of (cooked) rice risotto or two minute noodles, add the sauce, then warm in the microwave as necessary. (Another quick sauce can be made from a can of tomato soup mixed with sour cream, then thinned with water or stock.)

Liven up the skin of a cooked chicken by arranging the pieces, skin side up, in a foil-lined shallow baking pan. In a small saucepan or microwave bowl, heat together the juice of a lemon, 1 Tbsp melted butter and 1 tsp each of paprika and cumin. Brush over the chicken and heat until bubbly under a preheated grill. Don't overdo it, or the chicken will dry out. Serve with your favourite bread and a tomato salad.

Brush with butter and lemon juice without seasoning, then sprinkle with one of the interesting seasoning mixtures now available commercially, developed for microwave and regular oven use, eg., Tandoori, Enchilada, Oriental and French chicken seasonings. Such mixtures add interesting flavour quickly and, when used with restraint, are a boon for the 'short-order' cook. Of course you can heat these coated chicken pieces in the microwave too.

For another 'hurry up' treatment, mix in a fairly large, non-stick frying pan, ½ tsp cornflour, 1 tsp instant green herb stock (or ½ tsp salt), ¼ cup white wine, ¼ cup water and 1 tsp butter. As soon as this mixture boils and thickens slightly, turn the cooked chicken pieces in it and reheat them with the pan lightly covered. In another pan saute some sliced mushrooms briefly. Spoon mushrooms over chicken.

For something really easy, toss together boneless strips of chicken, with a spoonful of pesto and some strips of roasted red pepper (also from the deli) with a little mayonnaise. Serve in split pita breads, french bread or crusty rolls.

For creamy chicken on pasta, cook fresh fettuccine noodles in one pot, and saute some sliced mushrooms in a little butter or oil in a non-stick pan. Add a 425g can of your favourite condensed "cream of chicken and mushroom soup", ¼ cup milk, water or sherry, and ¼ cup sour cream. Bring this to the boil, take off the heat and stir in pieces of smoked or rotisseried chicken and the drained fettuccine.

For a quite different approach, shred the cooked chicken into a serving dish and toss with a little lemon juice and Mexican Seasoning (page 32). Serve surrounded by bowls of shredded lettuce, grated carrots, grated cheese, chopped fresh coriander leaf, sour cream and bought, or home-made, tomato salsa. Add a basket of warmed flour tortillas (now available in most supermarkets) and let your guests assemble their own delicious (and easy!) chicken burritos. (Or replace soft tortillas with crisp taco shells.)

chicken
under wraps

Now that packets of flexible flat breads are readily available at most supermarkets, we can have fun rolling and folding up all sorts of chicken mixtures in them. These edible packages can be enjoyed as appetisers, snacks, light meals, party food, or an easy, casual meal at the end of a busy day.

The various flat breads available may be called tortillas, mountain bread, naan, etc. Don't be puzzled by the different names – as long as the contents of the packages are thin and flexible, just take a packet home and experiment with it. You won't ever need to waste the contents if they won't roll up properly – just brush each piece very lightly with oil and perhaps a little Mexican or Cajun seasoning, cut it into rectangles or wedges, and bake at about 150°C until lightly browned and crisp. Use these as you would crackers and corn chips – they are especially good with dips.

Tortillas rolled or folded around fillings which have a Mexican flavour are many and varied, with names like tacos, burritos (see page 13), flautas, enchiladas and fajitas!

Chicken Quesadillas

Chicken quesadillas are the Mexican equivalent of thin, toasted cheese sandwiches. Brush 2 flour tortillas lightly with oil. Place one, oiled side down, in a medium-hot frypan. Spread with a little Salsa Fresca, (page 29) or other tomato salsa, sprinkle generously with grated cheese, and add some leftover cooked chicken, then top with the remaining tortilla, oiled side up. When the bottom has browned and the cheese melted, slide the "sandwich" out of the pan onto a board or plate, then flip it over and brown the other side. Cut in wedges and serve warm.

Wraps

Tortillas wrapped around non-Mexican fillings are known as wraps. Anything goes in these! In our house they are served for quick and popular lunches. Our fillings often contain cooked chicken from the refrigerator. Some of our favourites are:

- warmed shredded Chicken and Rice (page 24) with coriander leaves and an Indian chutney;
- Moroccan Chicken (page 36) with couscous and some chopped lettuce;
- Easy Oriental Simmered Chicken (page 40) with rice, beansprouts and a little hoisin sauce; or,
- Butter Chicken (page 41), rice and thinly sliced cucumber with a dash of mango chutney.

Warm tortillas by placing one or two at a time in a plastic bag and microwaving for 10-15 seconds or until pliable. Working quickly (to prevent bread drying out), place the prepared filling in the centre, fold the bottom up, over it, then wrap up from one side to the other. Wrap firmly in a paper napkin or in foil, crimping edges, if you think the filling could otherwise drip! Eat immediately, starting at the top, rather like eating an icecream in a cone.

Salad Rolls

Large square flat breads make wonderful salad rolls. We like the flat bread spread with cream cheese, mayonnaise or leftover satay sauce, with shredded lettuce or cabbage, grated carrot and cheese on this, and small amounts of cooked chicken, dried fruit, chopped nuts, etc. added for variety. Wrap long rolls in cling film and refrigerate until firm and cold, then unwrap and cut into manageable lengths.

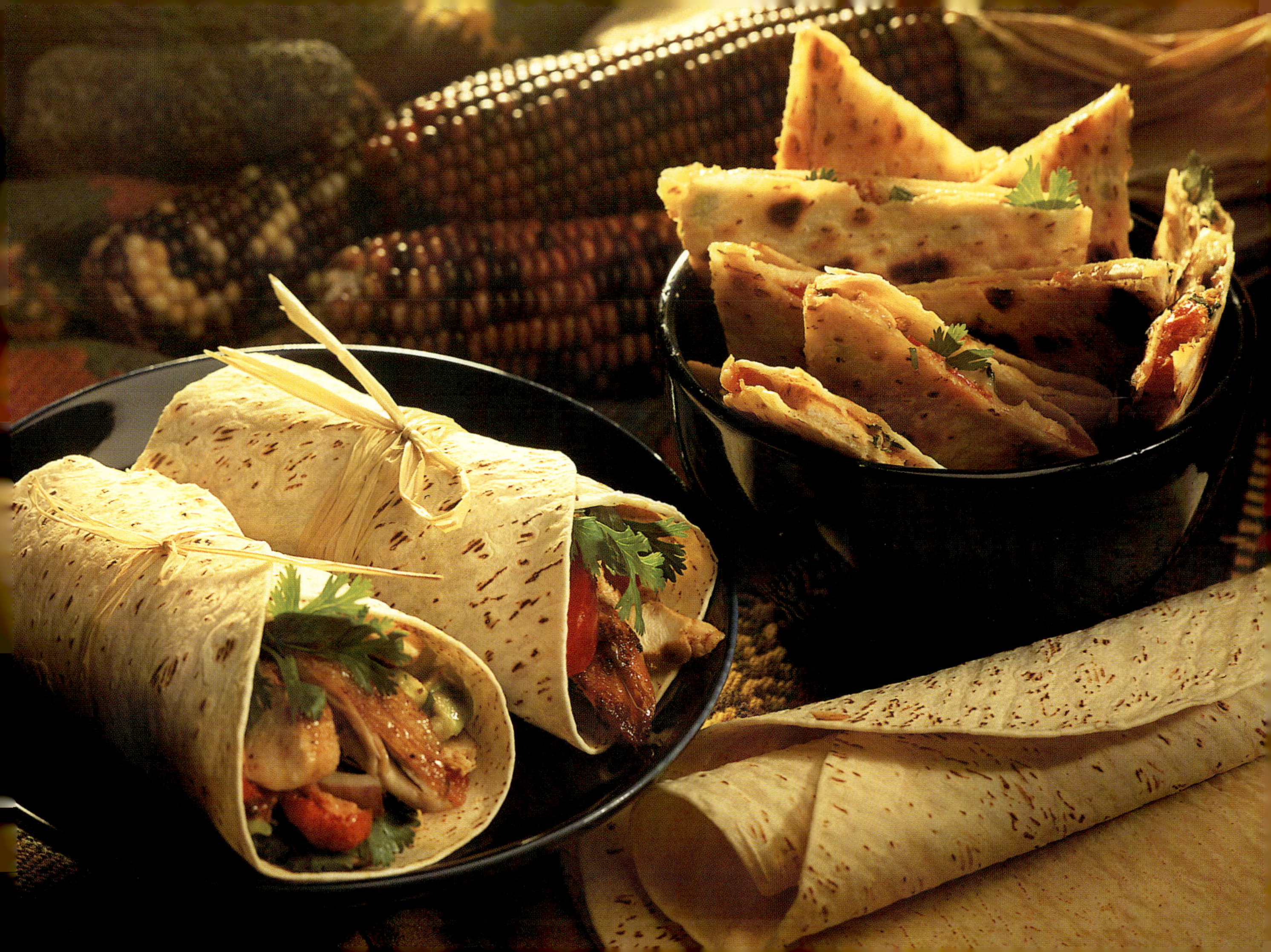

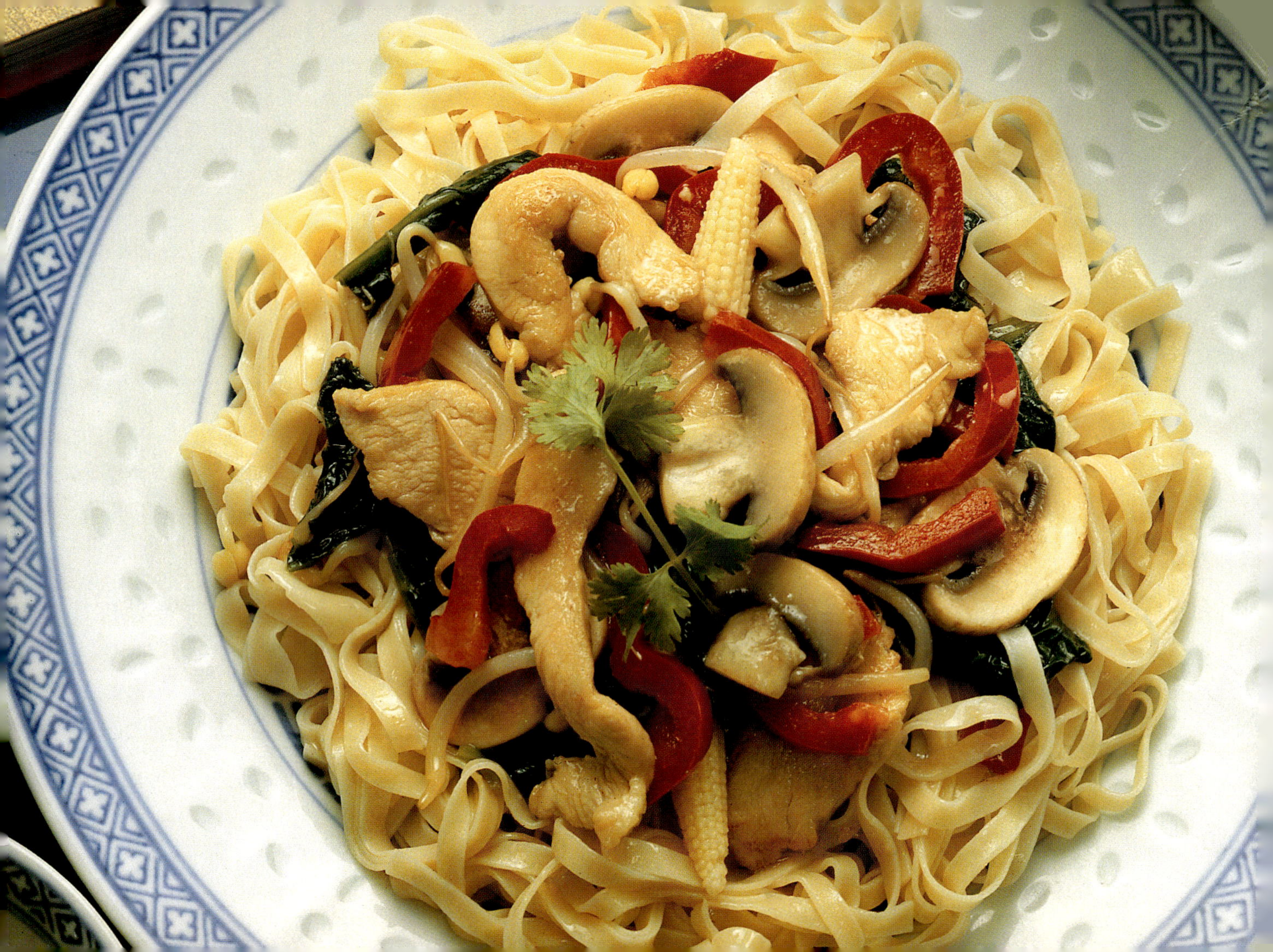

stir-fried
chicken

Once you get used to stir-frying chicken and vegetables, you will find this one of the fastest and tastiest meals you can make. The marinade flavours and glazes the chicken pieces and the vegetables are brightly coloured and tender-crisp.

FOR 2 SERVINGS:

- 200–300g boneless, skinless breast or thighs
- 1 tsp grated root ginger
- 1 clove garlic, sliced (or ½ tsp minced garlic)
- 1 Tbsp light soy sauce
- 1 Tbsp sherry
- 1 tsp brown sugar
- 1 tsp instant chicken stock or ½ tsp salt
- 2 tsp cornflour
- 2–3 cups prepared vegetables *
- 2–4 tsp oil
- 1–2 Tbsp water

* Use two or more of these quick cooking vegetables, eg. spinach, mushrooms, celery, cauliflower, zucchini, broccoli, spring onions, green and red peppers.

Cut the chicken breast meat across the grain into 5mm thick slices. Put into a plastic bag with the next 7 ingredients. Knead bag lightly to combine thoroughly and leave to stand for at least 15 minutes.

Slice the vegetables into pieces about the same size as the chicken. Heat half the oil in a large frypan or wok, over a very high heat. Add the prepared vegetables and toss until coated with oil and heated through. Add 1–2 tablespoons water, cover and cook until the vegetables are tender-crisp, then remove from pan and keep warm.

Add the remaining oil to the pan or wok if it seems dry, then stir-fry the chicken in its marinade, over a very high heat until the strips turn white, (probably about 2 minutes). Return the vegetables to the pan, toss gently to mix, warming the vegetables through if necessary.

Serve straight after cooking, on noodles or rice.

Microwaved Rice:
For 2 servings, put ½ cup of long-grain rice in a microwave dish with 1 cup of boiling water and ¼ tsp salt. Cover and microwave at 70% power for 10 minutes, then leave to stand for 5 minutes.

(For 4 servings, use 1 cup rice, ½ tsp salt and 2–2¼ cups boiling water. Cook at 70% power for 12–15 minutes, then stand for 5 minutes.) Use more water and longer time for softer rice.

Jasmine rice is especially good with Chinese food, and Basmati rice with Indian recipes.

spiced chicken and tomatoes

Ring the changes with this easy but tasty chicken and tomato mixture. Serve it as it is, on rice or add pasta or beans. Whichever you choose, you will finish up with a trouble-free dinner for two.

FOR 2 SERVINGS:

- about 500g bone-in chicken pieces (nibbles, drumsticks or thighs)
- 2 tsp oil
- 1 large onion, chopped
- 1 tsp minced garlic
- ½ tsp minced chilli or chilli powder
- 1-2 tsp ground cumin
- ½ tsp oreganum
- 425g can tomatoes in juice
- 1 cup water
- ½–1 tsp salt
- 2 tsp brown or white sugar
- 1-2 cups sliced zucchini, sliced green beans or broccoli
- 1 cup frozen or fresh corn kernels (optional)

Basic Recipe

Brown chicken evenly in a non-stick pot or frypan. Add onion and cook until lightly browned, then stir in the garlic, chilli, cumin and oreganum. Cook about 30 seconds longer.

Add the tomatoes, water, salt and sugar. Cover and simmer for about 20 minutes or until the chicken pieces are almost cooked. Add the vegetables of your choice and cook 10 minutes longer. If using fresh corn, remove the husks and silk, then cut the kernels off the cob. As the "rafts" of kernels cook, they separate.

Use this basic recipe in one of the following three ways:

Spiced Chicken on Rice. Thicken the sauce slightly, using a little cornflour mixed with water. Serve straight away or reheat when required. Spoon the mixture over plainly cooked rice (see page 17) in bowls. Top with chopped spring onions or coriander leaves.

Spiced Chicken and Pasta. Add 2 extra cups of water and the larger amount of salt to the recipe above. When the chicken and tomato mixture has simmered for 10 minutes, add 150g large macaroni or other pasta. Stir at intervals so pasta cooks evenly. Add vegetables 10 minutes after adding pasta. Taste and adjust seasoning if necessary, add a little extra boiling water if mixture seems dry. Serve, topped generously with chopped parsley. For best flavour, serve soon after cooking.

Spiced Chicken with Beans. After adding tomatoes etc, simmer with the smaller amount of salt for 15 minutes, then add a can of kidney beans (and its liquid), or a can of chilli beans. Add the green vegetables and/or corn only if desired. Simmer for 15 minutes longer. Check that everything is cooked and adjust seasoning. Serve immediately or reheated, in bowls, alone or on rice. Top with sour cream and grated cheese if desired.

"souped-up" chicken casseroles

As a young mother, I found these easy recipes useful! When expecting company for dinner I could assemble any in a few minutes, then feed, bathe and put the children to bed (before tidying the house!) knowing dinner was taken care of.

THESE RECIPES MAKE 3–4 SERVINGS EACH

For each recipe use 4 chicken quarters or about 1.2–1.5kg bone-in chicken pieces.

For Curried Pineapple Chicken
- 2–3 tsp curry powder or Indian curry paste
- ½ cup water
- 1 packet (about 30g) onion soup mix
- 1 can (about 225g) sliced pineapple (in juice)
- red pepper, chopped, optional

For Sherried Chicken & Mushrooms
- 1 packet (about 30g) mushroom soup mix
- ¼ cup sherry
- 1 cup water
- ½ tsp dried tarragon or thyme

For Fruity Chicken Casserole
- 2 tsp dark soy sauce
- 1 tsp minced garlic
- 1 packet (about 30g) onion soup mix
- 1½ cups apple and orange juice

General Method

Turn oven to 190°C, or 180°C for fan-bake.

Put the chicken pieces and all the ingredients (for any one casserole!) in an unpunctured roasting bag, then knead the bag gently to mix everything. Lay the bag flat, on a shallow baking pan with the chicken in one layer, best side down. Fasten the bag loosely with a twist-tie or string, leaving a finger-sized hole for steam to escape.

Bake for 30 minutes, then take the pan out and flip the bag over so the best side is now up. Cook 40 minutes longer. (Don't worry if the upper side of bag looks dark brown — the chicken inside should not burn.)

When the chicken feels tender (press through the bag), take out of oven and let cool a little. Before serving, thin the sauce with a little boiling water, if necessary.

Curried Pineapple Chicken. Serve on rice (see page 17) with one or more salads.

Sherried Chicken & Mushrooms. Just before serving, mix in ½–1 cup sliced, sauteed mushrooms, and 2–3 Tbsp of cream, if you like. Serve on fresh fettuccine with broccoli.

Fruity Chicken. Serve on rice with a green or mixed salad or with mashed potatoes, green beans or broccoli.

chicken
paprikash

When you need to brighten up a cold and miserable day, treat yourself to this delicious, creamy chicken mixture served over pasta ribbons or other large pasta shapes. Use low-fat sour cream if your conscience bothers you – the sauce will still taste very good!

FOR 3-4 SERVINGS:

- 1 tsp olive oil
- 2 Tbsp butter
- 1 medium onion, diced
- 300–400g boneless, skinless chicken breasts, cut crosswise into 1cm slices
- 1 medium green or red pepper, sliced
- 2 Tbsp paprika
- ½–1 teaspoon caraway seed
- ½ cup dry white wine
- 400g fresh pasta
- 1 cup sour cream
- 1 Tbsp tomato paste
- 1 teaspoon salt
- black pepper to taste
- chopped fresh parsley to garnish

Heat the oil in a large frypan, then add the butter. Add the diced onion and cook until the onion softens. Stir in the chicken pieces and sliced green or red pepper. Sauté until the chicken has lost all its pink colour and the vegetables are tender-crisp, about 5 minutes.

Add the paprika and caraway seed to the pan and sauté for about 1 minute more. Stir in the wine, then reduce the heat and simmer gently for about 5 minutes, stirring and scraping the bottom of the pan occasionally. (Put the pasta on to cook during this time.)

Stir in the sour cream, tomato paste, salt, and black pepper. Reduce the heat to low and simmer for 2 to 3 minutes more.

Drain the cooked pasta and toss with a little extra butter or olive oil. Arrange on individual plates or a serving platter. Top with the sauce and serve immediately, garnished with a little chopped parsley.

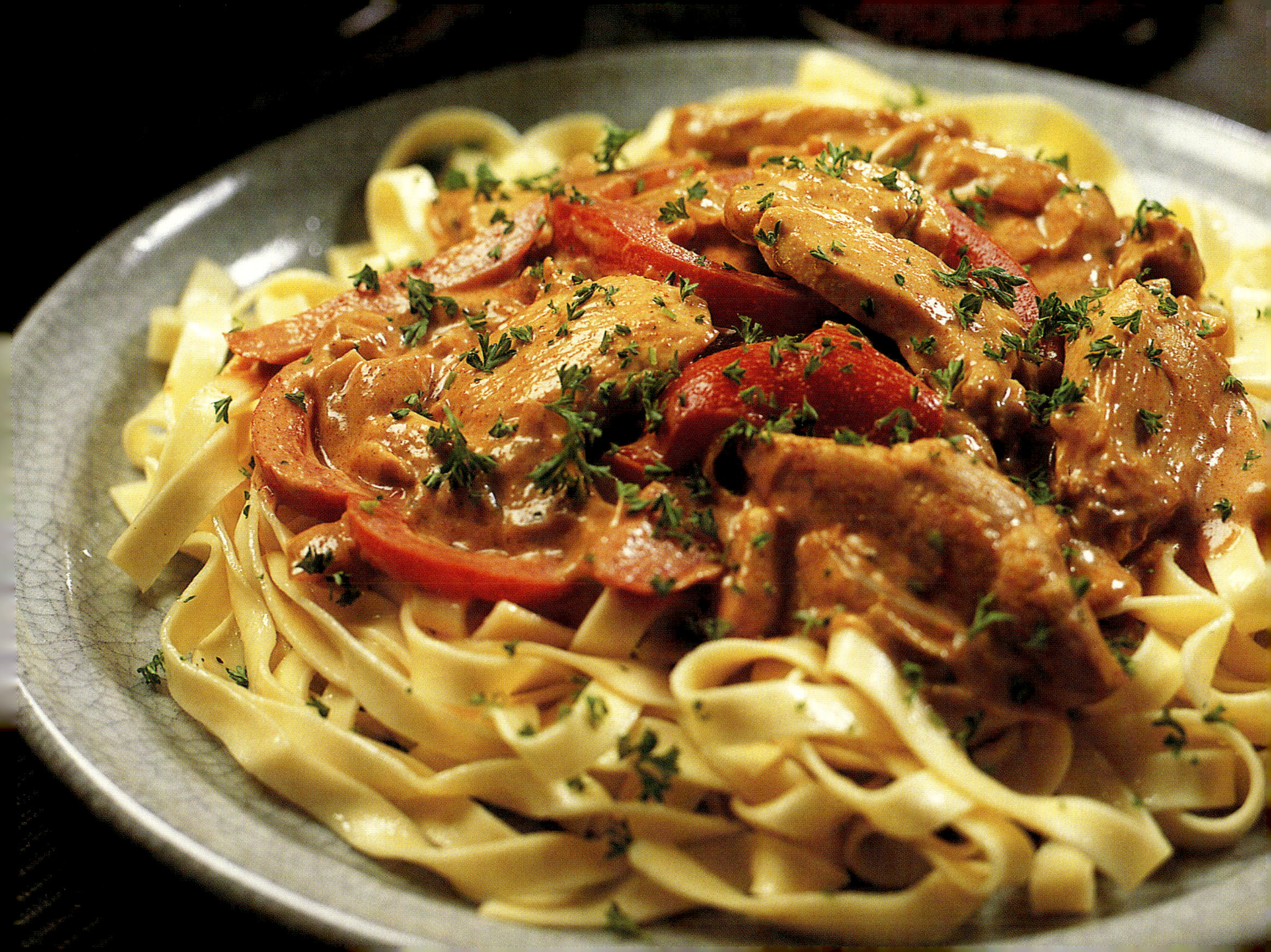

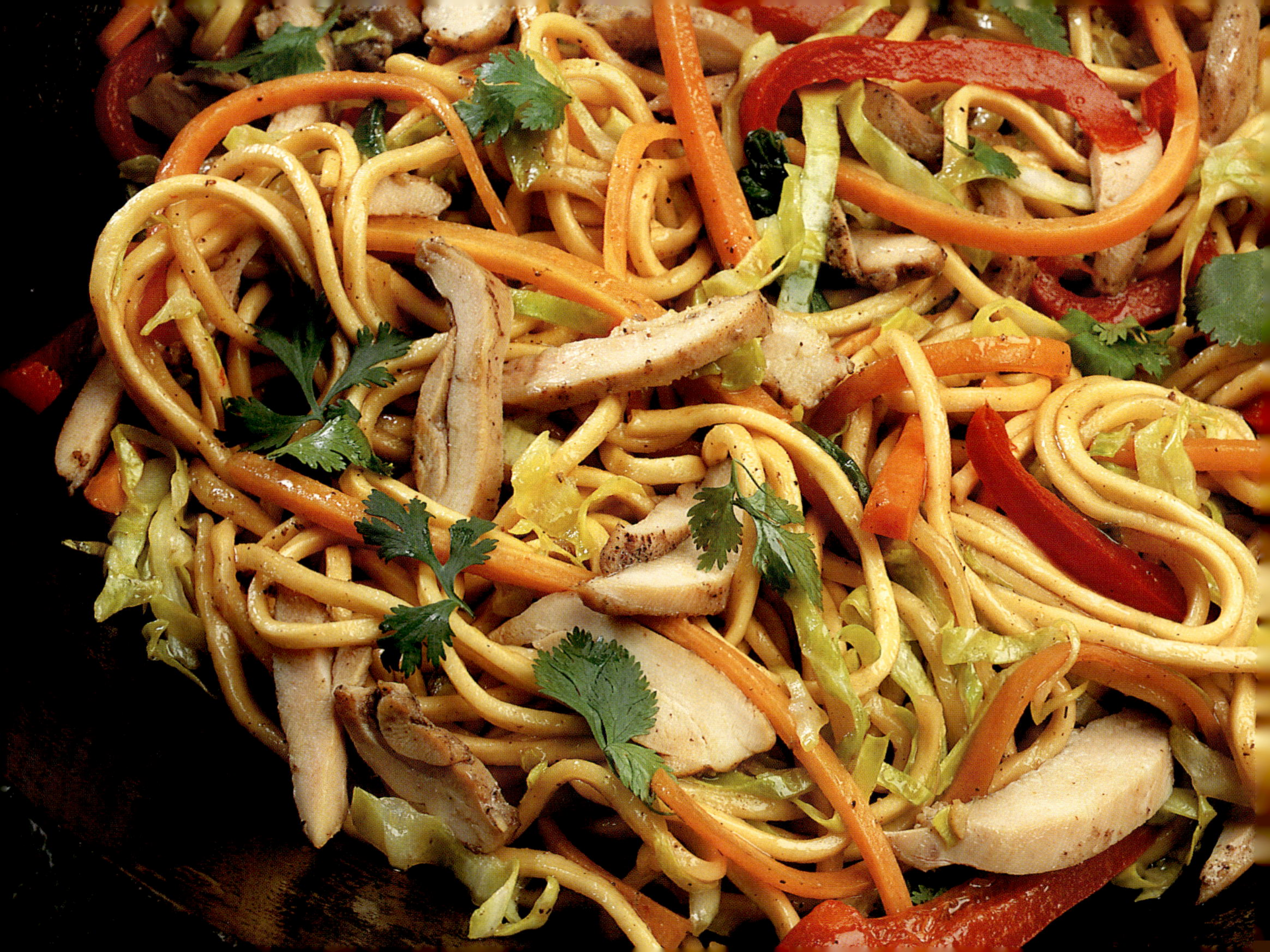

five-spice chicken with fresh noodles

Fresh noodles are available in most Asian food stores – they are delicious when cooked with this five-spice flavoured chicken and vegetables. For best flavour, serve as soon as the vegetables are tender, straight after cooking.

FOR 3-4 SERVINGS:

- about 400g boneless, skinless chicken breasts or thighs
- 2 Tbsp each light soy sauce and sherry (or lemon juice)
- 2 tsp dark sesame oil
- ½ tsp five-spice powder

- 2 cloves garlic, peeled and chopped
- 3 spring onions, sliced
- 1 large carrot, cut into matchsticks
- 1 medium red pepper, thinly sliced
- 2 cups thinly sliced cabbage
- 2–3 Tbsp chopped fresh coriander
- 3 Tbsp canola or other oil
- 500g fresh egg noodles
- ½ cup water
- 2 Tbsp each light soy sauce and hoisin sauce
- ½ tsp sugar

Cut the chicken into bite-sized cubes or slices, then mix with the soy sauce, sherry, sesame oil and the five-spice powder. Cover and leave to stand for at least half an hour. (The marinated chicken can stand for up to 24 hours if refrigerated.)

Prepare the next six ingredients as described, before you start any cooking. (Do not mix them.)

Heat the oil in a large wok or pan, add the marinated chicken and the garlic and stir-fry over a high heat until the chicken is lightly browned on all sides. Add the spring onions, carrot, red pepper and fresh noodles. Reduce the heat, then add the water, soy and hoisin sauces and sugar. Toss everything together, then cover and leave to simmer for 5 minutes, stirring once or twice.

Stir in the sliced cabbage and coriander leaf, and add ¼ cup of additional water if the mixture looks too dry. (It should have a nice moist gleam, but should not be swimming in liquid.) Cover and cook for another 2 minutes.

Serve immediately, garnished with some additional coriander leaf and a handful of bean sprouts.

VARIATION: Replace fresh noodles with 250g (dry weight) of egg noodles or spaghetti, cooked until just tender.

baked chicken & rice dinner

This easy recipe makes one of my favourite chicken dinners. It looks after itself as it cooks, tastes wonderful and the ingredients can be varied.

FOR 4 GENEROUS SERVINGS:

- 8 bone-in chicken pieces (1-1.5kg) or a whole chicken of the same weight, quartered
- 1 Tbsp olive or canola oil
- 1–2 onions, chopped
- 2 carrots, quartered lengthwise, then chopped
- 1½ cups long-grain rice
- 1–2 tsp chopped garlic
- ½–1 tsp minced chilli (from a jar)
- 1–2 tsp ground cumin
- 1 tsp oreganum
- 3½ cups boiling water
- 2 tsp salt
- 1–2 cups chopped beans, zucchini, broccoli or other green vegetables
- paprika and extra cumin

Turn the oven on to 210°C, or 200°C for fan-bake, and select a baking or roasting pan just big enough to hold the chicken in one layer. Pat the chicken pieces dry, and brown them on both sides in the oil in a large, preheated frypan. Meanwhile, prepare the onions and carrots.

Put chicken aside, and put the chopped onions, carrot and the rice in the pan. Cook over moderate heat until rice is milky white. Stir in the garlic, chilli, cumin and oreganum, then cook for 1 minute longer. Add the boiling water and salt, then pour the mixture into a non-stick baking or roasting pan about 24 x 30cm. Stir the green vegetables into the rice, then arrange the chicken pieces on top, best side up.

Sprinkle chicken with a little extra cumin and paprika. Bake uncovered for 50–60 minutes until rice is tender (with all the liquid absorbed) and the chicken juices run clear when pierced to the bone. Serve immediately.

VARIATION: Other vegetables, (eg. celery, pumpkin, mushrooms, cauliflower) may replace those listed. Heat long-cooking vegetables with the rice and add quicker cooking vegetables later. Change amounts and varieties of spices and herbs if desired.

NOTE: If the chicken pieces do not cover all the rice in your baking pan, place foil over uncovered rice (but not over the chicken).

grandma's whole chicken pot roast

Vegetables and herbs flavour this old fashioned "chicken dinner in a pot". If you find carving daunting, cut the cooked chicken into chunky pieces with kitchen scissors!

FOR 4 SERVINGS:

- 1 fresh or thawed chicken, about 1.4–1.8kg
- 1 Tbsp oil
- 1 onion, chopped
- 2 cloves garlic, chopped (optional)
- fresh thyme, parsley and/or other fresh herbs
- 2 bay leaves
- 1 cup chicken stock (page 61) or 1 tsp instant stock powder in 1 cup water
- ½ cup white wine or water
- 8 small potatoes
- 3 medium carrots, in chunky pieces
- 2 rashers of bacon, if available
- about 2 cups prepared beans, zucchini, broccoli or frozen peas
- 2 Tbsp cornflour plus ¼ cup water
- chopped parsley

Cook this in a large (flameproof) cast iron casserole if you have one. If not, brown the bird in a frypan, then transfer to a large, non-flameproof casserole.

Heat the oven to 180°C, or 170°C for fan-bake.

Pat the chicken dry and brown the breast and back in the oil in the flameproof casserole or frypan. Put aside. In the remaining oil, lightly brown the onion and garlic. Tie together two bundles of herbs, each containing some thyme, parsley, other fresh herbs and a bay leaf. Put one of these inside the chicken and place it in the casserole on a Teflon liner or a folded piece of baking paper. Arrange the onion mixture and the second herb bundle around the chicken.

Add the liquids and the prepared potatoes and carrots. Place the bacon rashers over the chicken breast if you are using them. Cover the casserole and bake for 45 minutes, then add the prepared green vegetables, cut in regular sizes so they will cook evenly. Cover and cook for another 30 minutes, until the chicken is tender and the vegetables nicely cooked. While these cook, mix 2 Tbsp cornflour to a thin paste with ¼ cup cold water in a cup or small bowl and chop the parsley.

Working quickly, divide the cooked vegetables between 4 serving bowls. Lift the chicken onto a board, cut into 4 pieces with kitchen scissors or carve it into chunky pieces. Place these on top of the vegetables. Heat the cooking liquid (removing herb bundle) and stir in enough of the cornflour paste to thicken it as much as you like. Add the chopped parsley and spoon the sauce over the chicken and vegetables.

VARIATION: If you are using a cast iron casserole, you may cook the whole thing on top of the stove instead of in the oven. The cooking time will be the same.

30 minute
chicken dinner

This recipe is good when you want a meal on the table in 30-40 minutes from the time you first think about it. Make it for two or three people in a large covered frypan on the stove-top, or make double the recipe in a larger electric frypan. (Leftovers reheat well.)

FOR 2-3 SERVINGS:

- 4–6 boneless skinless chicken thighs
- flour to coat
- 2–3 tsp olive or canola oil
- 2 large cloves garlic, finely chopped
- 1 tsp ground cumin
- 2 tsp oreganum
- ½ tsp thyme
- ¾–1 tsp salt
- ⅛–¼ tsp chilli powder
- ½ cup orange juice or white wine
- ½ cup water
- 6–9 small potatoes, scrubbed and halved
- 8 small or 2 large carrots,
- 1 stalk celery, sliced (optional)
- 1–2 cups chopped green beans, zucchini or broccoli florets
- ¼ cup finely chopped parsley

Dry chicken thighs with paper towels, then turn in flour and brown on both sides in the oil in a large (preferably non-stick) frypan, over fairly high heat. Lower heat, add the chopped garlic, dried herbs and salt. Add chilli powder to suit your taste. The smaller amount should be acceptable for young children. Add the orange juice (or other fruit juice or white wine) and water, turn the chicken so all sides are seasoned and cover the pan.

Add the prepared potatoes and carrots (in small enough pieces to cook fast), then chop the celery (if available) and prepare the green vegetables. Add to pan, and turn the chicken, potatoes and carrots, adding more water if sauce has boiled down and thickened too much. Cook about 10 minutes longer, until all vegetables are tender, and the chicken has cooked for about half an hour altogether.

If necessary, thin cooking liquid with more water, or thicken by cooking it uncovered for a few minutes. Taste and adjust seasoning if necessary.

Sprinkle generously with chopped parsley or other fresh herbs and serve in shallow bowls, with warmed bread rolls.

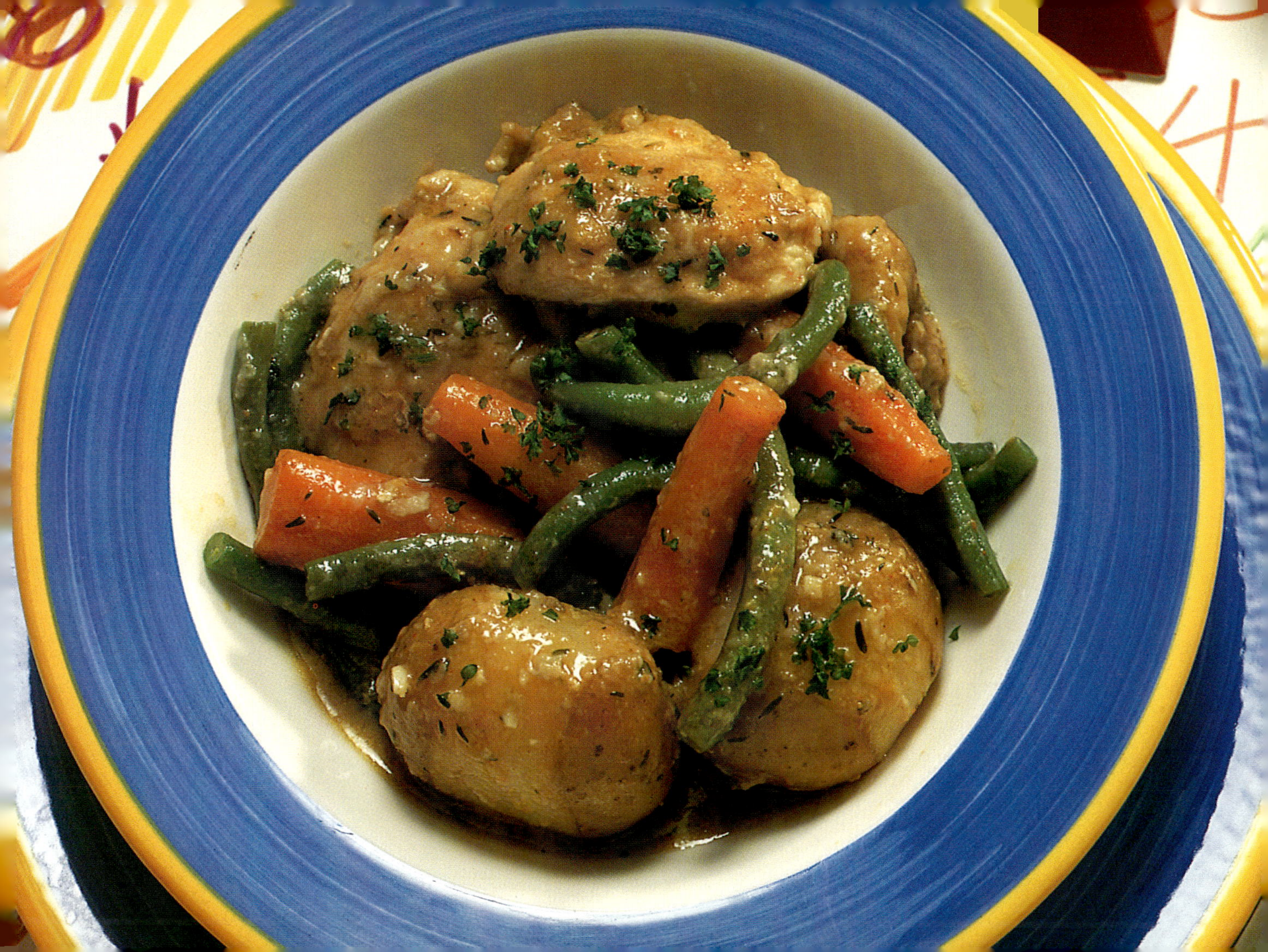

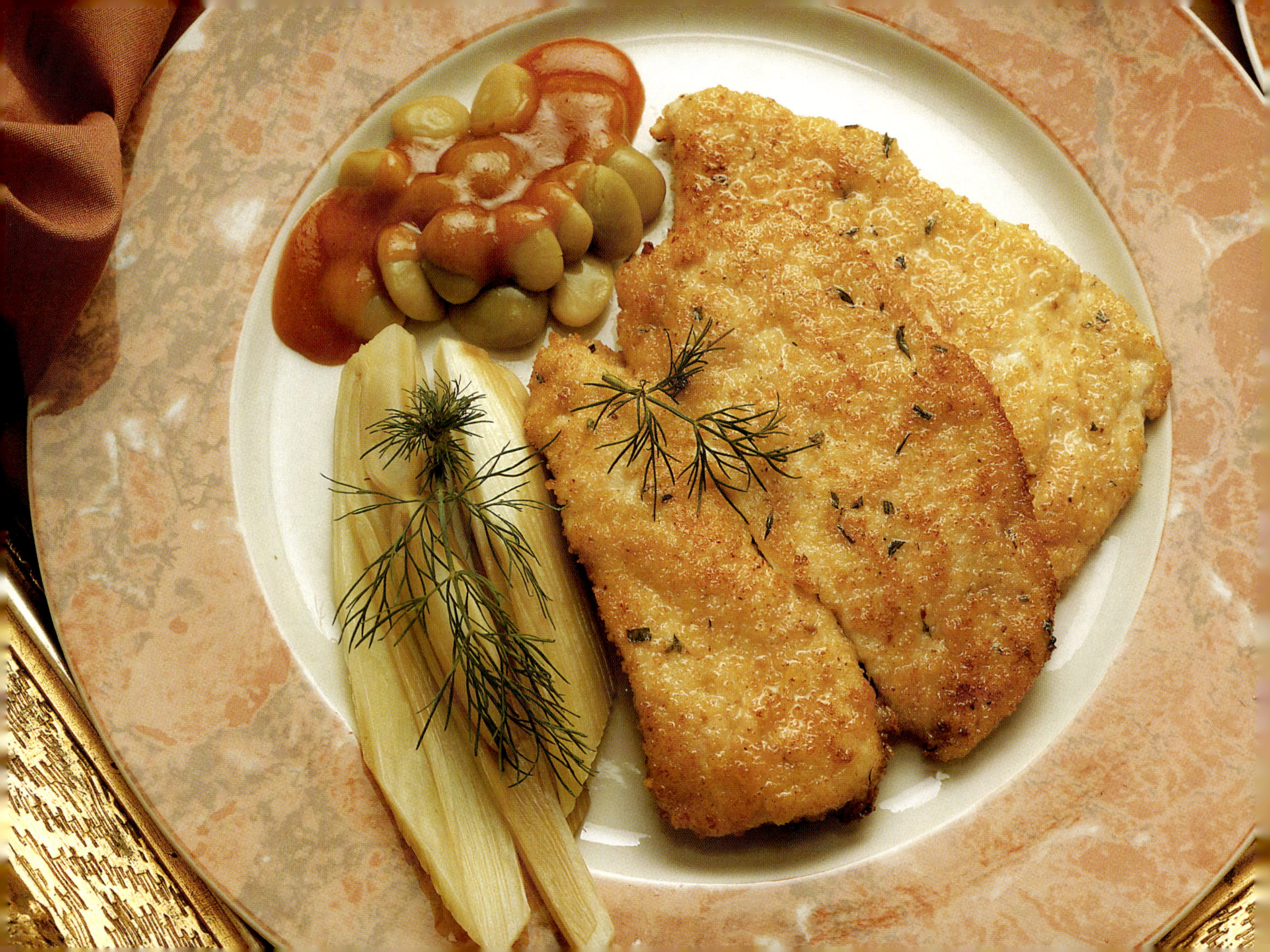

chicken breasts
florentine

When making this quickly cooked recipe, you can work ahead if you like. The coated, uncooked chicken may be kept in the refrigerator for up to 24 hours before cooking.

FOR 2 SERVINGS:

- 2 boneless, skinless chicken breasts (200–250g)
- 2 Tbsp grated Parmesan cheese
- 2 Tbsp dry breadcrumbs
- 1–2 tsp finely chopped fresh herbs, including sage if possible
- about ¼ cup milk
- about 1 Tbsp oil
- about 1 Tbsp butter

Put one boneless, skinless chicken breast between two sheets of plastic. Using a rolling pin, bang evenly and gently until the breast is of even thickness and about double its original length and width. Repeat with the second.

Mix together the Parmesan cheese, breadcrumbs and herbs. Dip each piece of chicken first in a shallow container of milk, then in the cheese mixture, patting the coating thoroughly onto the chicken with your fingers. Refrigerate between plastic until required, or cook immediately.

Heat the oil and butter in a large (preferably non-stick) frypan. When hot, cook the chicken over a high heat for about 1 minute a side, until coating is golden. Do not overcook or the chicken will be dry. Serve immediately with a salad and bread or with one or more hot vegetables. Salsa (see below), although not traditional, is delicious served with chicken.

VARIATION: If you like several smaller pieces of chicken on a plate, cut each flattened chicken breast into two or three, before coating and cooking, or use the same weight of chicken tenders instead, flattening them very lightly.

Easy Salsa Fresca
Stir together the following seasonings in a bowl: ½ tsp each ground cumin, oreganum, salt, and sugar. Stir in 1–2 Tbsp chopped pickled Jalapeno peppers or ½ tsp minced chilli, and a very finely chopped garlic clove (optional). Chop 4 large red tomatoes (discarding seeds), 1 ripe avocado, ¼ of a red onion or 2 spring onions, and several coriander sprigs. Fold gently but thoroughly into the mixture in the bowl. Leave for half an hour if possible, then taste, adding extra salt and sugar if necessary.

pat's cuban chicken

One of my favourite occupations is swapping recipes with good cooks. The friend who gave me this recipe tells me it is Cuban, and is very popular with her teenage sons, as well as being a great hit with her guests. Reading the ingredients list was enough to make my mouth water!

FOR 4 SERVINGS:

- 4 skinless, boneless chicken breasts
- 3 cloves garlic, finely chopped
- 1 tsp ground cumin
- ¼ tsp dried oreganum
- ¼ tsp dried thyme
- 1 Tbsp finely chopped fresh coriander leaves
- 3 Tbsp lime juice
- 3 Tbsp olive oil
- 1 tsp sugar
- ½ tsp salt

Pat chicken breasts dry with a paper towel, trim if necessary, then place one breast between a folded plastic bag, on a board. Bang evenly and gently with a rolling pin until breast is one and a half times its original size and of even thickness. Place in a sponge roll tin big enough to hold all of the chicken in one layer. Prepare the other breasts in the same way.

Mix the remaining ingredients together in a screw-topped jar, or combine them using a food processor. Brush mixture over both sides of the prepared chicken, and leave to marinate for at least 15 minutes, or up to 24 hours in the refrigerator, covered with plastic.

Preheat a heavy frying pan or barbecue plate until very hot, brush or rub with a film of oil, then cook the chicken until brown on each side and just cooked in the middle. This should take only 2 minutes per side if you have beaten the chicken out evenly.

Serve alone, or with a salsa (below), a bread roll or rice (page 17), and a salad.

Salsa is a wonderful accompaniment for any plainly cooked chicken.

Mango Salsa
Mix together in a bowl: 1 Tbsp lemon (or lime) juice, ½ tsp minced red chilli, ½ tsp salt, 1–2 Tbsp chopped coriander leaf. Then fold in: 400g can mango slices, drained and chopped, or 1 cup finely chopped fresh mango, ¼ cup finely chopped spring onion. Leave to stand for at least 15 minutes, then add salt and pepper to taste, if necessary.

Kiwifruit Salsa
Mix together in a bowl: 1 finely chopped clove of garlic, ½ tsp ground cumin, 3 Tbsp lime or lemon juice, ¼–½ tsp minced chilli, and ½ tsp salt. Chop, then fold in: 4 large ripe kiwifruit, 2 spring onions or shallots, about ¼ red pepper and 2–4 stalks of fresh coriander or basil. Leave for 15 minutes, then taste, adding sugar if necessary.

quick chicken
satay sticks

When strips of breast meat are threaded on skewers, they keep their shape during cooking and look more exotic when served. This is a good way to turn a couple of chicken breasts into a quick, interesting meal.

FOR 2 SERVINGS:
- 2 boneless, skinless chicken breasts
- 1–2 Tbsp lemon or lime juice
- 1 Tbsp each soy sauce and fish sauce
- 1-2 tsp sesame oil
- 1 tsp ground cumin
- 2 cloves garlic, finely chopped
- 1 tsp grated fresh ginger
- 1 Tbsp chopped coriander leaves (optional)

Soak 10–12 bamboo skewers in cold water.

Cut each chicken breast into 5 or 6 strips. Place the strips in a bag with all the ingredients.

Leave to marinate from 5 minutes to 24 hours, as time allows. Thread the chicken strips lengthwise onto the skewers and grill or barbecue close to the heat until cooked, 3-5 minutes each side. (Juice should run clear when chicken is pierced.)

Serve on rice (see page 17) with warm (bought or home-made) satay sauce (see below) and a cucumber or other salad.

Quick Satay Sauce
- 1 onion, chopped
- 1 clove garlic, chopped
- 2 Tbsp oil
- ½ tsp minced chilli or chilli powder
- 2 tsp brown sugar
- 1 tsp grated fresh ginger
- 1 Tbsp soy sauce
- 2 Tbsp lemon juice
- ½ cup peanut butter
- about ½ cup water
- leftover chicken cooking juices from above
- salt to taste

Heat the onion, garlic and oil in a medium size pan over moderate heat until the onion is transparent. Stir in the next 6 ingredients. Add the water and any remaining marinade and cooking juices. Bring to the boil. Season to taste with salt. Thin to pouring consistency with extra water. Refrigerate leftovers, thinning with extra water before serving.

mexican chicken

All boneless, skinless chicken cuts are delicious when coated with the Mexican seasoning used in this recipe. Whether you grill, barbecue or microwave your chicken, we are sure you will find this a popular and useful recipe.

FOR 4 SERVINGS:

- about 500g boneless chicken (use boneless, skinless thighs, breasts or tenders)
- 2–3 tsp canola or other oil
- 2 Tbsp Mexican Seasoning (see below)

Mexican Seasoning
- 1 Tbsp paprika
- 1 Tbsp oreganum
- 1 Tbsp ground cumin
- 1 Tbsp onion or garlic salt
- 1 Tbsp flour
- 2 tsp caster sugar
- ½-1 tsp chilli powder

Bang chicken breasts between 2 pieces of plastic until they are 1cm thick, using a rolling pin. When using thighs, if necessary, snip the flesh in places, to make sure they will lie flat when cooked. Chicken tenders should not need any attention. Brush both sides of the prepared chicken lightly with oil.

Prepare the Mexican Seasoning by mixing all the ingredients in a screw topped jar.

Sprinkle both sides of the chicken with the Mexican Seasoning, using quantities to suit your taste. About 2 teaspoons per breast or thigh gives a good flavour. Use less for tenders. (Store extra Mexican Seasoning in a screw topped jar for later use.)

Grill or barbecue close to the heat. Chicken is cooked when juices no longer run pink when pierced deeply in the thickest part.

Microwave pieces in one layer in a covered dish, to the same stage, allowing, at 50% power, about: 1½ minutes per thigh; 2 minutes per breast; or, 45 seconds per tender.

Serve with corn on the cob, tomatoes, bean salad or green salad, or shred for use in tacos, burritos, wraps (see page 14) etc.

VARIATION: If you find this Mexican seasoning too hot, use less chilli in your next batch rather than using the mixture too sparingly, since the other flavourings are interesting but not hot.

teriyaki chicken

This chicken has an appetising brown glaze and may be cooked in a microwave oven or baked conventionally. For easy clean up, it is marinated and cooked in a tough oven-proof bag.

FOR 2 SERVINGS:

- 400–500g chicken wings, nibbles or drumsticks
- 2 Tbsp Kikkoman soy sauce
- 2 Tbsp sherry
- 1 Tbsp brown sugar
- 1–2 garlic cloves, crushed (optional)
- 1 tsp grated fresh ginger
- ½ tsp cornflour (if microwaving)

Put chicken pieces in an unpunctured oven bag with the remaining ingredients. Squeeze air from bag and leave to marinate at least 15 minutes, but preferably for an hour. Secure bag loosely with a rubber band leaving a finger-sized steam hole. Position bag so it is flat with chicken pieces in one layer, with the thicker ends nearest the outside.

Microwave on high power turning over once, for 7–9 minutes, depending on size and initial temperature of chicken pieces. Stand for 3–4 minutes. Chicken is cooked when juices run clear, not pink, when pierced to the bone at the thickest part. If necessary, microwave for longer.

Alternatively, omit cornflour and bake in bag with loose twist-tie, at 190°C for about 45 minutes, turning once. Test as for microwaved chicken.

While hot, turn pieces in sauce, then remove from the bag. The glaze dries as pieces stand for a few minutes. Serve hot, with remaining glaze spooned over chicken if desired. Serve on rice (see page 17) with stir-fried or plainly cooked vegetables.

VARIATION: For Sesame-Soy Chicken, use dark soy instead of Kikkoman soy, add 1 Tbsp sesame oil and omit ginger. Cook as above, then sprinkle with 2 Tbsp sesame seeds while the glaze dries.

country captain
chicken

This American recipe has been made regularly in our house for thirty years. Whenever we serve it for friends, they tell us how much they enjoy it and go home with the recipe. Alter the seasonings to suit your taste.

FOR 6 SERVINGS:

- about 12 bone-in chicken pieces
- ½ cup flour
- 3–4 Tbsp oil
- 1 large onion, sliced
- 1 clove garlic, sliced
- 1 green pepper, sliced
- 1 Tbsp brown sugar
- 2–3 tsp curry powder
- 1 tsp salt
- ½ tsp thyme
- 425g can whole tomatoes in juice
- ¼ cup currants

Pat the chicken pieces dry with paper towels, coat them evenly with flour, then heat the oil in a large frypan and brown over high heat, turning pieces when necessary. Remove from the pan.

Lower the heat and add onion, garlic and green pepper. Cook 2–3 minutes until onions are transparent but not browned, then replace chicken pieces in the pan, skin side down. Stir in the sugar, curry powder, salt and thyme, then add the roughly chopped canned tomatoes. Cover and cook over a low heat for 15 minutes. Turn chicken (so the most attractive side is up), add currants and cook for a further 10–15 minutes, or until juices run clear.

VARIATION: For larger numbers, arrange browned chicken pieces best side down in a roasting pan lined with baking paper or a Teflon liner. Prepare the remaining ingredients in a frypan, as above, then pour over the chicken. Cover with foil and bake at 180°C, or 170°C for fan-bake, for 30 minutes, then uncover, turn and cook 15–30 minutes longer until the juices run clear when thick pieces are pierced deeply. (If the chicken and sauce are prepared ahead and refrigerated before baking, allow 15 minutes extra cooking time.)

Serve on rice (see page 17) with a leafy green salad or with broccoli or green beans.

chicken & vegetable curry

This South-East Asian curry is a great way to turn frozen chicken pieces into a really interesting meal! Don't be put off by the long list of ingredients - most of the additions are spices that are all added at once.

FOR 3-4 SERVINGS:

- 2 Tbsp canola or olive oil
- 1 Tbsp curry powder (mild or hot)
- 1 tsp ground turmeric
- 4–6 whole cloves
- 3–4 cm piece cinnamon stick (or ½–1 tsp ground cinnamon)
- 1 large onion, very finely diced
- 1 clove of garlic, chopped
- 2 Tbsp finely chopped fresh ginger
- 500–700g small chicken pieces (drumsticks, wings or nibbles)
- 3–4 small potatoes, cubed
- ¾ cup chicken stock (or water)
- ¾ cup coconut cream
- 1–2 cups green vegetables (frozen peas or beans, broccoli, zucchini etc.)
- ½–1 tsp salt
- 1–2 Tbsp chopped fresh coriander (optional)

Heat the oil in a large (preferably non-stick) pan, add the curry powder, turmeric, whole spices and the onion, garlic and ginger. Cook, stirring frequently, until the onion is soft and beginning to turn clear.

Add the chicken pieces and continue to cook, stirring at regular intervals, until the chicken is lightly browned on all sides. Stir in the cubed potatoes, chicken stock (or water) and coconut cream. Allow the mixture to come to the boil, then reduce the heat and simmer until the potato is tender and the chicken is cooked through. If you want the sauce thin, cover the mixture and simmer it gently, or if you want a thicker mixture, simmer it uncovered, boiling a little more vigorously.

Cut the vegetables into bite-sized pieces, then add these to the mixture and simmer for a few minutes longer until the vegetables are just cooked. Add salt and coriander (if using) to taste, then serve as is or over rice. (If you can find them at your supermarket, fresh or frozen naan bread or roti also make an ideal accompaniment.)

NOTE: You can vary the `hotness' by using hot or mild curry powder. (Most supermarkets now have both.)

moroccan
chicken

In Morocco this dish is made with preserved, salted lemons, but fresh lemons are just fine! While the flavour may not be quite the same it's still delicious. Make this for friends if you are looking for something a little different.

FOR 4 SERVINGS:

- 1 large onion
- 3–4 cloves garlic
- 3 Tbsp olive oil
- 1 Tbsp tomato paste
- 1 tsp ground cumin
- 1 tsp paprika
- ½ tsp ground ginger
- ½ tsp salt
- 2 Tbsp chopped coriander leaves
- 2 lemons
- 4 large bone-in chicken pieces or 8 drumsticks
- 15–20 black olives

Chop the onion and garlic finely, using a food processor if available. Add the next seven ingredients and the juice of one of the lemons and mix into a thick paste.

Place the chicken into a large shallow casserole dish and spread the paste mixture evenly on all sides of the chicken. Cut the remaining whole lemon lengthwise into eight wedges. Place between pieces of chicken with the olives.

Cover and leave to stand for 1–2 hours if possible (or leave overnight in the fridge). When ready to cook, heat oven to 180°C, or 170°C for fan-bake. Cover loosely with foil and bake for 30 minutes, then cook uncovered for another 30 minutes.

VARIATIONS: For a less lemony flavour use strips of lemon rind instead of lemon wedges. Replace lemon wedges with the skin of one preserved, salted lemon, if available.

Serve with rice (see page 17) or couscous and a green salad.

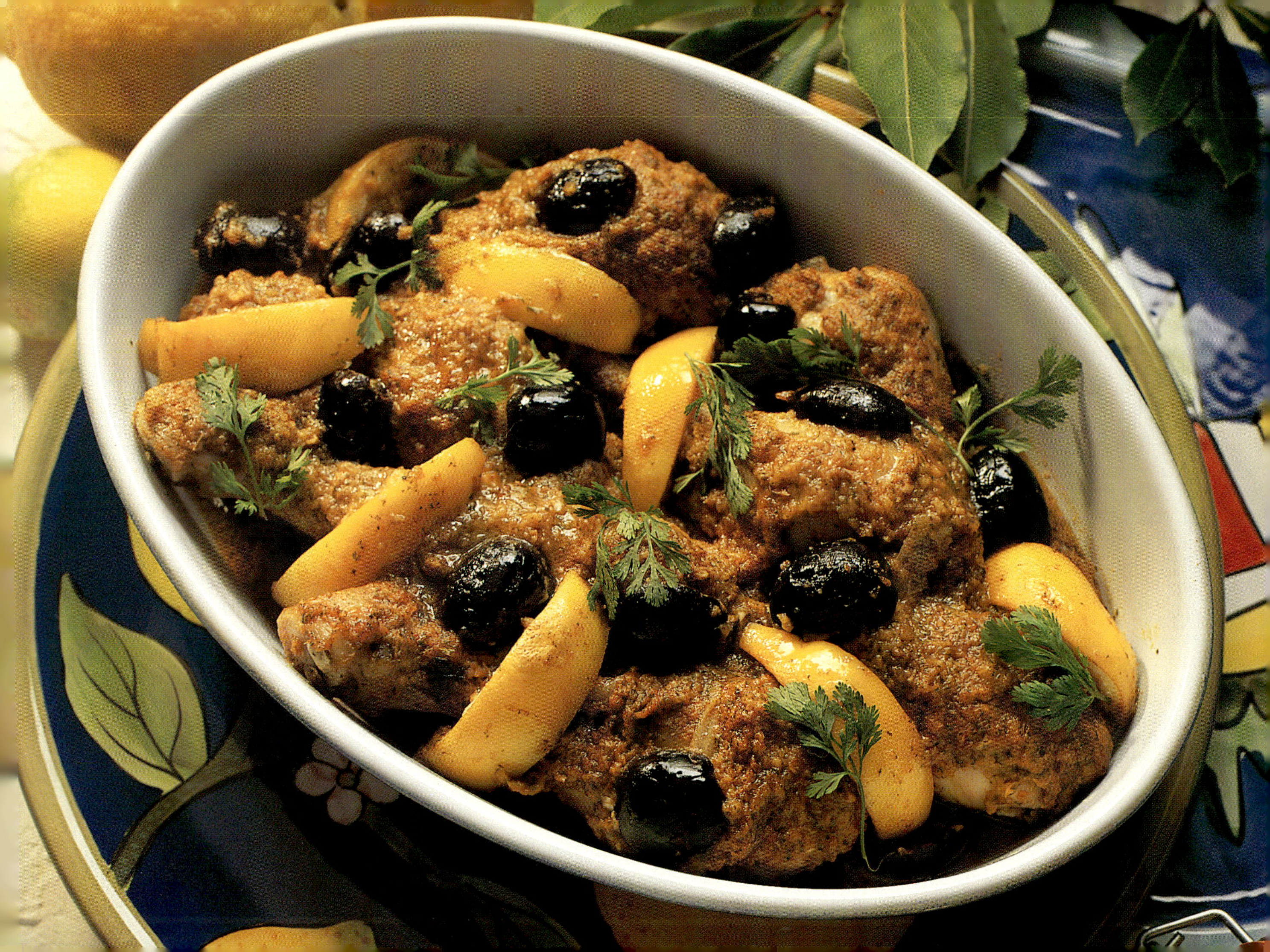

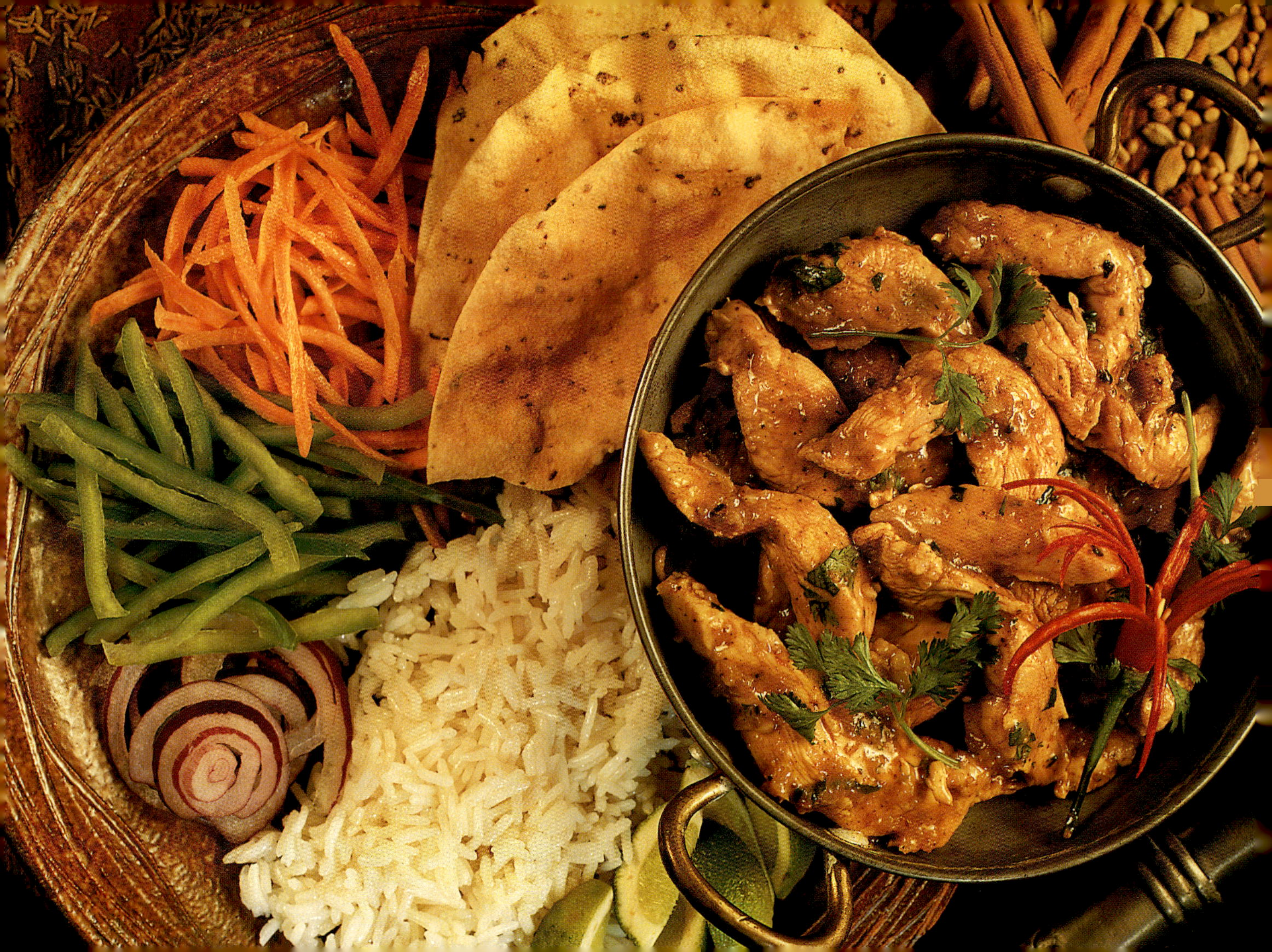

balti
chicken curry

This curry is made very quickly using tender, boneless chicken which needs very little cooking. Although this recipe is made with commercially mixed curry mixtures instead of a home-prepared Balti curry paste, it still seems popular. If you can find a Balti curry paste on sale, try it instead.

FOR 2 SERVINGS:

- 300g boneless, skinless chicken breasts or thighs
- 1–2 Tbsp oil
- 2 cloves garlic, finely chopped
- 1 large onion, finely chopped
- 2 tsp good quality hot Indian curry paste* or curry powder
- ½ cup chicken stock or water
- 1–2 tsp garam masala
- 1 Tbsp chopped fresh coriander leaves
- salt to taste

* Prepared Indian curry pastes can now be found in many supermarkets.

Cut the chicken into crosswise strips about the thickness of a pencil. In a wok or large frypan, heat the oil over a medium heat and cook garlic very briefly (about 30 seconds). Add the onion and cook until lightly and evenly browned, about 4–5 minutes. Add the curry paste or powder, stir over moderate heat for 2–3 minutes, then add the chicken. Raise the heat and stir-fry until the chicken loses its raw look, for about 3–5 minutes.

Add the chicken stock (or water) and simmer, stirring, on a lower heat for 5 minutes. Test a piece of chicken to check that it is cooked right through. If not, cook for a few minutes longer. Add the garam masala and coriander. Mix to combine well, add salt to taste, and serve immediately.

Serve with rice, (see page 17) poppadums and your choice of other curry accompaniments.

NOTE: The flavour and hotness of the curries you make depends a lot on the curry paste or powder you use in them. After you have used the product you have bought a few times, you should know how much suits you, per serving. Keep to these proportions whatever recipes you make using the same commercial product. Be prepared to experiment a little, until you reach this stage.

easy oriental simmered chicken

Here is an unusual, very popular and easy recipe, originally from an American friend with Korean parents. It is flavoured with star anise, a spice available from stores (or specialty departments) which stock ingredients for Asian cooking.

FOR 4-6 SERVINGS:

- 8-12 bone-in chicken pieces
- ½ cup light (or Kikkoman) soy sauce
- 1 Tbsp honey
- ¼ cup brown or white sugar
- 1 cup water
- 2 Tbsp grated root ginger
- 2 or 3 cloves garlic, crushed
- 3–6 petals star anise (depending on the strength you like)
- 2 Tbsp sherry
- 4 spring onions, chopped
- cornflour to thicken

Put the pieces of chicken in a pot (preferably a stovetop-to-table variety) with all the ingredients except the spring onions and cornflour.

Bring to the boil, then simmer on a very low heat for 45–60 minutes, or until the chicken is tender, turning the pieces once or twice. Add the chopped spring onions and thicken the liquid as desired, with cornflour mixed to a paste with cold water.

Serve immediately on plainly cooked rice (or reheated when required). A salad of coarsely chopped crisp (iceberg) lettuce tossed in sesame dressing is very nice with this.

Sesame Dressing
Combine in a screw-topped jar: 1 Tbsp sesame oil, 2 Tbsp canola oil, 2 Tbsp sugar, 2 tsp salt, 4 Tbsp cider vinegar, ¼ tsp black pepper, 2 Tbsp freshly toasted sesame seeds. Shake just before using.

VARIATION: Star anise is one of the spices in 5-spice powder. If necessary, replace the star anise in this recipe with ¼–½ tsp 5-spice powder.

simon's butter chicken

Butter chicken is justifiably popular, in Indian restaurants and from supermarket freezers. This easy, home-made version of butter chicken is quick, simple and delicious, and actually contains no butter!

FOR 2-3 SERVINGS:

- 2 Tbsp canola or other oil
- 1 medium onion, finely diced
- 2 cloves garlic, peeled and chopped
- 2 tsp curry powder (mild or hot according to taste)
- 1 tsp each ground cumin, coriander and ginger
- 250–300g boneless, skinless breasts or thighs, cubed
- 425g can tomatoes and onion OR whole tomatoes in juice
- 1–2 tsp garum masala
- ¾ cup plain unsweetened yoghurt
- ¼–½ cup cream
- 1–2 Tbsp chopped coriander leaf, fresh or bottled

Heat the oil in a large pan, then add the finely diced onion and chopped garlic. Cook, stirring frequently, until the onion is soft and clear but has not browned (about 5 minutes). Add the curry powder, cumin, coriander and ginger, and cook, stirring constantly for about a minute longer.

Cut the chicken into bite sized cubes, then add to the pan. Cook, stirring occasionally until the chicken has lost its pinkness, then stir in the canned tomato mixture. Allow the mixture to boil, then reduce the heat to a gentle simmer and cook for 8–10 minutes, or until the chicken is cooked through.

Stir in the remaining ingredients and reheat without boiling. Serve over steamed rice (see page 17), accompanied with poppadums and/or naan bread. (Naan is now available frozen in many supermarkets.)

VARIATION: For an extra smooth sauce, replace the can of tomatoes and onion (or whole tomatoes in juice) with a 300g can of condensed tomato soup, plus ½ cup of water and cook as above. (Tomato soup may sound like an odd addition, but it does work well!)

TIP: Poppadums "puff" nicely in the microwave – arrange 3 or 4 in a single layer over the paper towel covered carousel, then microwave on high for 1–2 minutes, turning once.

thai-flavoured **stir-fried** chicken

Now that Thai cooking has become popular, ingredients such as fish sauce, lemon grass (not called for in this recipe), chillis, coriander leaves and basil are available, not only fresh, but as semi-prepared, convenience ingredients.

FOR 4 SERVINGS:

- 400–500g boneless, skinless breasts or thighs
- 2 Tbsp oil
- 1 tsp finely chopped garlic
- 2 spring onions, chopped
- 1 Tbsp fish sauce or light soy sauce
- 2 Tbsp rice vinegar or wine vinegar
- ¼ tsp chilli powder or ½ tsp minced chilli
- 2 tsp sugar
- ¼ cup chicken stock (page 61) or 1 tsp instant stock powder in ¼ cup water
- 1 tsp cornflour
- 1–2 Tbsp Thai chilli sauce, optional
- 2–3 Tbsp fresh coriander leaf or basil, chopped (optional)

Slice each chicken breast crosswise, with your knife at an angle to the board, into about 8 slices.

Mix the sliced chicken with the oil, chopped garlic, spring onions, the fish sauce, vinegar, chilli and sugar. Heat a wok or large frypan, add the chicken mixture and cook over high heat, stirring all the time, for about 2 minutes, until the chicken is milky white, and has lost its translucency.

Remove the cooked chicken from the pan and keep it hot. Stir the liquid and cornflour together, add to the pan and stir until the sauce thickens and has boiled down to about half its volume, about 30 seconds.

Return the chicken to the pan, toss to coat with the sauce. Serve like this, or stir in the Thai chilli sauce. Toss with the chopped coriander or basil and serve immediately on rice (page 17), with a salad. (See Sesame Dressing, page 40.)

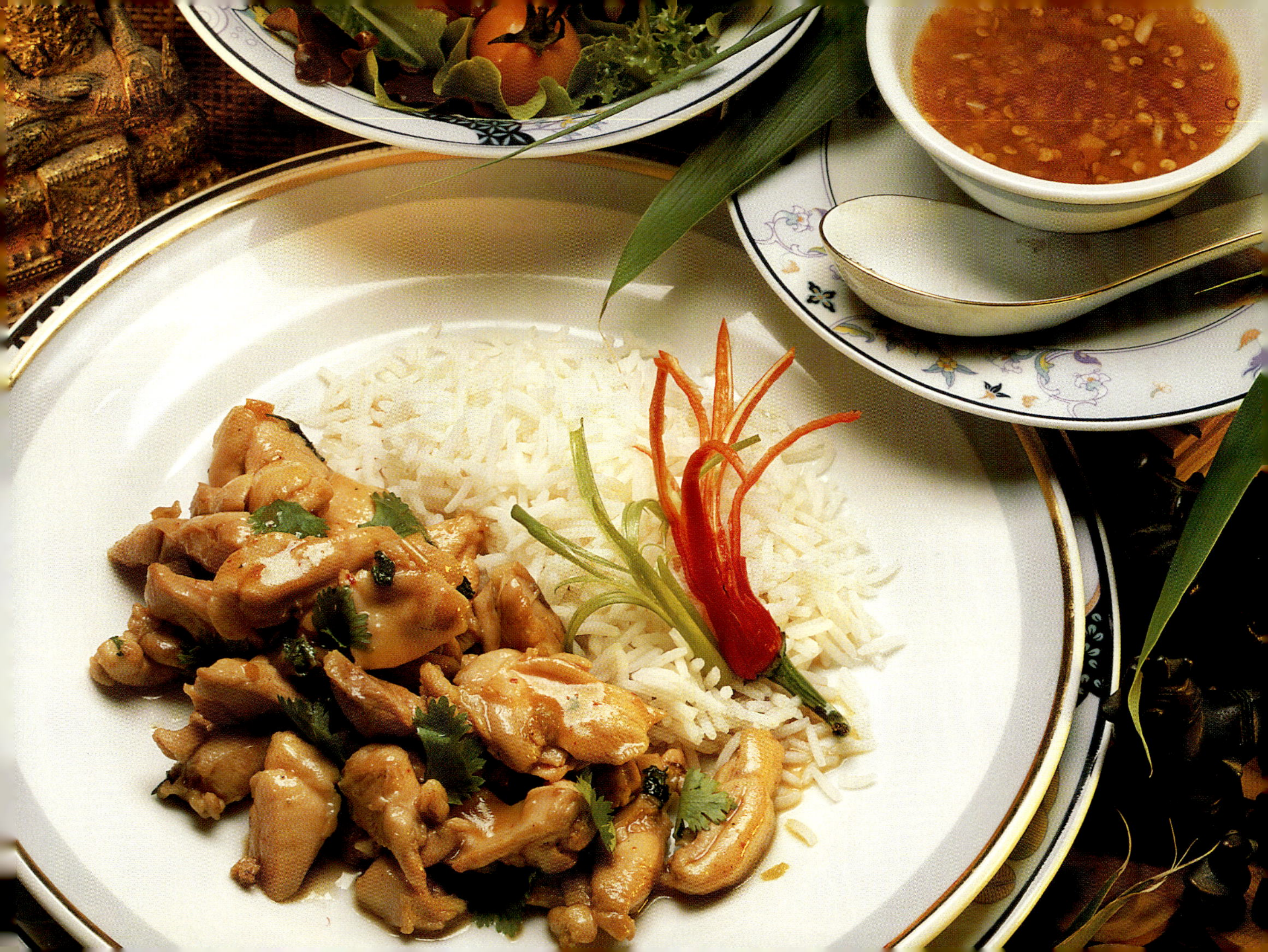

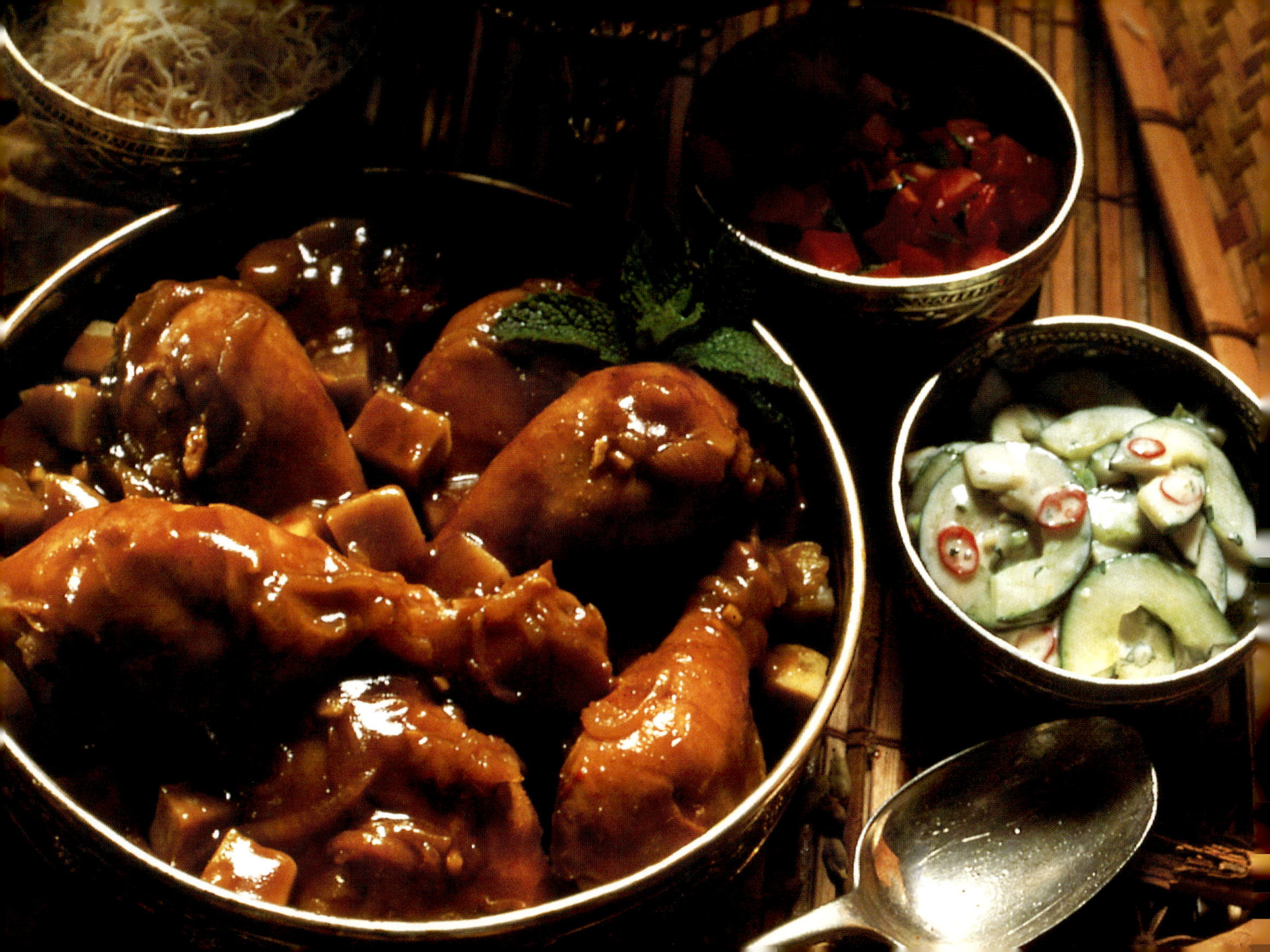

billy's special
chicken &
kumara curry

This delicious recipe was sent to me by a NZ woman whose family befriended a visiting Malaysian family. This mixture, made by one of the visitors, proved very popular when the families shared a meal. Don't leave out the extra spices — they make all the difference!

FOR 4-8 SERVINGS:

- 1–2kg chicken pieces or drumsticks
- 2–3 Tbsp oil
- 2–3 large onions, sliced
- 2–3 large cloves garlic, chopped
- 1 tsp salt
- 2 tsp sugar
- 4–6 tsp curry powder
- 3–4 cups water
- 12 star anise "petals"
- 1 cinnamon stick
- 10 cardamom pods (with seeds)
- 2–3 large kumara, in 2cm cubes

When two quantities are given, use the smaller amount when using less of chicken (or vice versa).

Use thawed or fresh chicken pieces or drumsticks. Pat dry if necessary. Heat oil in a large pot or pan, add prepared onion and garlic and cook over moderate heat until onions are fairly evenly browned. Stir in salt, sugar and curry powder and heat for a minute longer, stirring constantly.

Add the prepared chicken, brown lightly, then add the water.

Tie the remaining spices loosely in a piece of loosely woven cloth, put this in the liquid, cover and simmer for about an hour. Turn chicken pieces occasionally. Add the peeled, cubed kumara 15–20 minutes before the end of the cooking time. (The kumara thickens the sauce slightly.)

To serve, pile the chicken and kumara on generous amounts of rice and spoon the extra liquid over. If you like, serve green beans or a cucumber salad on the side.

NOTE: Star anise is a spice used in Chinese cooking. When seen whole it is most attractive, with about eight woody "petals", many of which contain a round seed. Together, these resemble a star or flower. The dried spice keeps well and it is worth finding a store selling oriental foods. If you cannot find this spice, replace it in this recipe with a teaspoonful of five-spice powder, a spice mixture that owes much of its flavour to ground star anise.

VARIATION: If preferred, bake at 180°C for about 1½ hours in a roasting pan covered in foil, adding kumara after 1 hour.

thai green curry

Although this recipe does require a few special ingredients, most of them keep well. Once you have them on hand, you will be able to use them to produce a variety of quick and delicious meals.

FOR 3-4 SERVINGS:

- 3–4 Kaffir lime leaves (fresh, frozen or dried), optional
- 2 Tbsp oil
- 1–2 Tbsp (bottled) Thai green curry paste
- 1 cup coconut cream
- 300–400g boneless, skinless chicken thighs or breasts
- 1 medium onion, sliced
- 2 Tbsp fish sauce
- 1 tsp sugar
- 2–3 zucchini, sliced
- ½ cup peas or green beans, fresh or frozen
- 150–200g can bamboo shoots, drained (optional)

Cover dried lime leaves with a little boiling water, and put aside to soak for a few minutes.

Meanwhile, heat the oil in frypan or wok. Stir in the curry paste and cook for 1–2 minutes, then add the lime leaves cut into 1cm slices.

Carefully pour in the coconut cream, and add the chicken pieces, cut into 2cm cubes. Add the onion, fish sauce and sugar and simmer for five minutes, stirring occasionally.

Add the vegetables, and bamboo shoots (if desired), and ¼ to ½ a cup of water to thin sauce if required. Simmer until chicken is cooked through and vegetables are just tender, about 10–15 minutes.

Serve in bowls, over fragrant Thai (Jasmine) rice (see page 17), garnished with chopped basil or spring onion, and with the curry accompaniments of your choice.

two-minute
chicken breasts

We have found that this wonderfully quick recipe seems popular with all age groups. Make it when you rush into the house after work, without the energy to cook anything elaborate or time-consuming.

FOR 2 SERVINGS:

Marinade
- 1 Tbsp sherry
- 2 tsp sesame oil
- 2 tsp brown sugar
- 1 clove garlic, finely chopped
- ½ tsp grated root ginger

- 3 chicken breasts (about 300g)
- 1–2 Tbsp oil
- 1 tsp cornflour
- 1 Tbsp sherry
- 1 Tbsp water
- chives, spring onions or coriander leaves

Cut each chicken breast crosswise into 6–9 pieces.

Mix together the first measure of sherry, the sesame oil, brown sugar, garlic and root ginger. Marinate the chicken pieces in this mixture for at least 5 minutes but preferably longer. (Refrigerate the chicken in its marinade in a plastic bag, if you like to work ahead and want an instant meal without any last minute chopping or grating.)

Heat the oil in a heavy non-stick pan, add the marinated chicken (and the marinade), and stir-fry for about 2 minutes, or until the chicken flesh is white (not pink) all the way through when cut.

Mix the cornflour, extra sherry and water, pour over the chicken and toss to coat with the lightly thickened liquid.

Serve immediately, sprinkled with chopped chives, spring onion, or fresh coriander leaves.

Serve with bread rolls and a salad or on rice (page 17) or noodles.

paprika **drumsticks**
with pan-baked scones

If I'd been given a dollar for every time I've cooked this chicken, I'd be rich! Good hot, warm or cold, it is reliably delicious! Of course you can cook the chicken without the scones, but the two are very good together — the scones are flavoured with the chicken drippings.

FOR 4-6 SERVINGS:

- 2 Tbsp butter
- 2 Tbsp oil
- 12 chicken drumsticks
- 2 Tbsp flour
- 1 tsp paprika
- ½–1 tsp curry powder
- 1 tsp garlic salt
- 1 tsp caster sugar

Heat the oven to 200°C, or 190°C for fan bake.

Melt the butter with the oil in a large roasting pan lined with a Teflon liner, baking paper or foil. (This ensures minimum clean-up later). Then turn the chicken pieces in it. Push coated chicken to one end of the pan. Mix the dry ingredients, then shake evenly through a small sieve over the chicken pieces, turning so all sides are coated. (Use all the mixture.)

Bake uncovered for 20 minutes, then turn. Five minutes later push chicken to one end, leaving the other end clear for scones. Add the scones (see below) then bake for another 15 minutes. (The chicken pieces are cooked when the juices at the thickest part run clear, not pink, when pierced to the bone.) If the chicken is cooked before the scones brown, remove from the pan.

Pan-Baked Scones
- 2 cups self-raising flour
- 25g butter, melted
- about ¾ cup milk

Measure the flour into a bowl. Melt the butter, remove from the heat and add the milk. Pour all the liquid into the flour and mix with a knife to a soft dough. (Add more flour or milk, if necessary.)

Roll dough out on a floured board, more thinly than normal. Cut into 12–16 round or square scones and turn in the buttery pan juices before placing fairly close together in one end of the roasting pan. Bake for about 12 minutes, until lightly browned top and bottom.

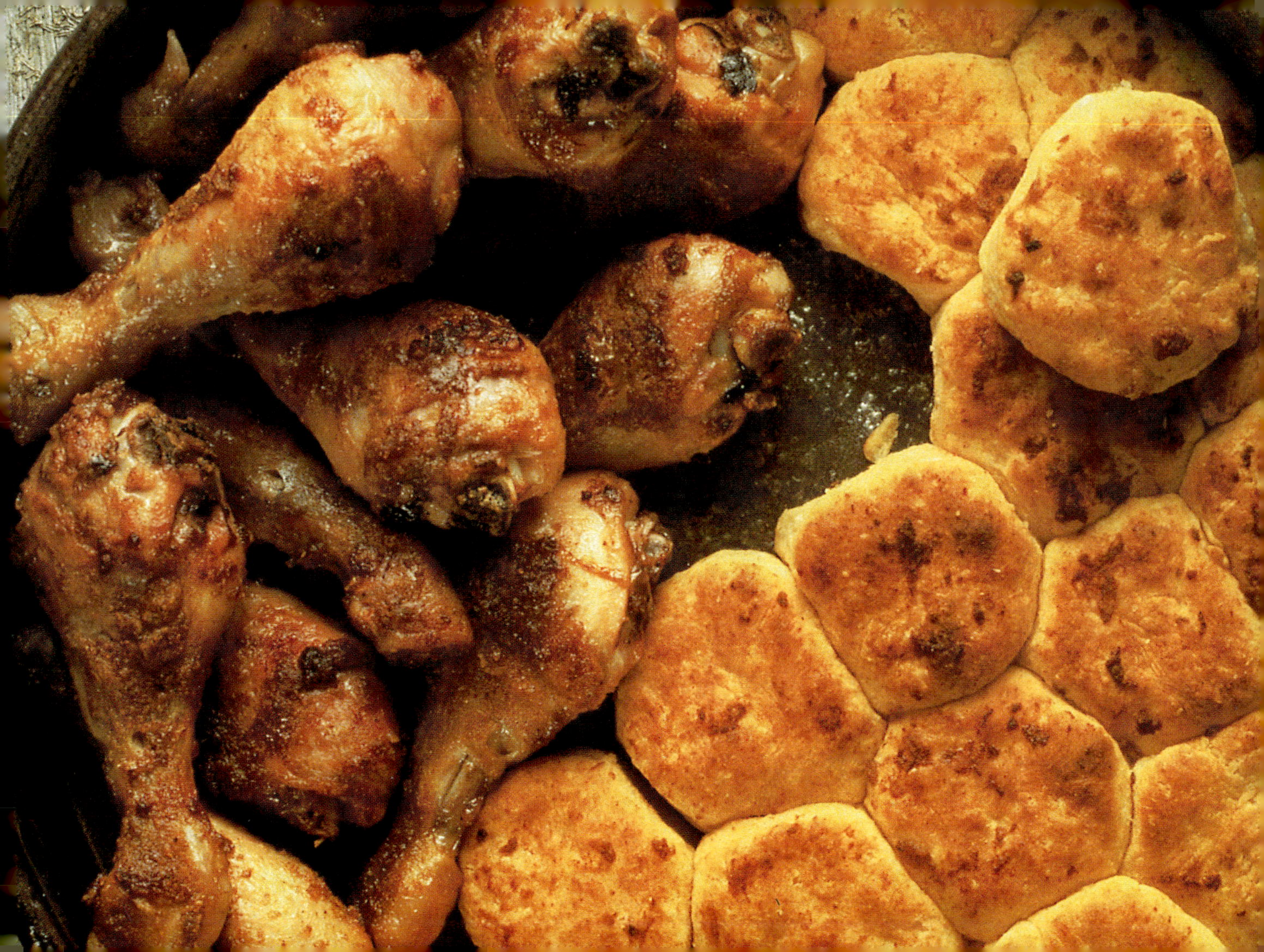

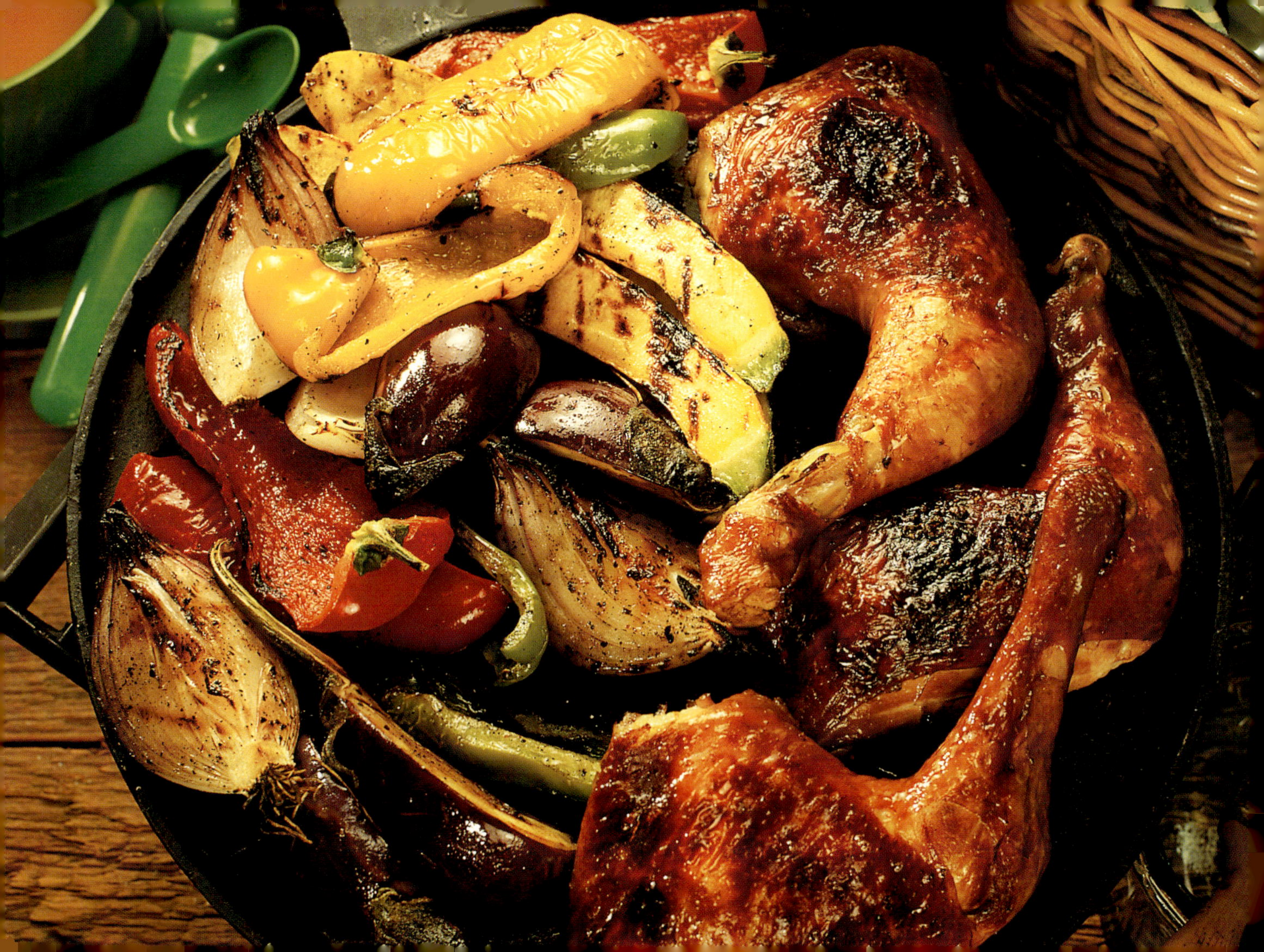

barbecued **red** chicken

Barbecued chicken with a difference! This chicken is precooked in a strongly flavoured sauce before it is barbecued or grilled. This means that not only is the cooking time reduced, but you don't have to worry about the outside of the chicken browning before it is cooked close to the bone.

FOR 4 SERVINGS:

- 4 chicken legs
- 1 cup cold water
- ½ cup dark soy sauce
- ½ cup light soy sauce
- 2 Tbsp sherry
- walnut sized piece fresh ginger, peeled and sliced
- 1 clove garlic, peeled
- 1 star anise "flower"
- 1½ Tbsp sugar

Pat the chicken legs dry with paper towels. Combine all the remaining ingredients in an unpunctured oven bag or a covered microwave dish, then add the chicken legs. Close the bag with a rubber band or piece of string, leaving a finger-sized hole through which steam can escape during cooking.

Microwave on High for 12–14 minutes, or until juices are no longer pink when thighs are pierced deeply. Turn pieces in the bag, or dish, 2 or 3 times so that all sides are flavoured by the marinade.

Or simmer the chicken legs in the marinade in a covered pan for 15–30 minutes, turning once or twice. Test as above.

Pour off cooking liquid, strain and refrigerate for re-use within a week, or freeze for up to six months if you want to use the liquid again for this recipe.

Barbecue or grill the chicken soon after precooking, or refrigerate until required. The chicken can be cooked quite close to the heat, as it is already cooked and needs only reheating.

Serve hot with barbecued fresh vegetables, warmed bread rolls and a leafy green salad, if you like.

Suitable vegetables for barbecuing include quartered red onions, quartered red, yellow or green peppers, mushrooms, halved or quartered small eggplant and green or yellow zucchini, halved lengthwise. Brush prepared vegetables with plain, herb or garlic-flavoured olive (or other) oil and barbecue or grill close to the heat, turning at intervals, until vegetables are tender, with some char marks, but not burnt. Allow 15–20 minutes for most vegetables.

"shortcut" barbecued chicken legs

When it's not warm enough to sit round in the garden, speed up the cooking by precooking chicken legs before you take them outside to barbecue. Offer a choice of pre-mixed glazes and serve the tasty, sizzling chicken only 10 minutes later.

- chicken legs, about 350g each
- soy sauce

Mustardy Citrus Glaze
- 1 Tbsp grainy mustard
- 2 Tbsp lemon or lime juice
- 1 tsp grated lemon or lime rind
- 1 Tbsp olive or other oil
- 1 large clove garlic, finely grated

Hot Sesame Glaze
- 2 Tbsp light soy sauce
- 2 Tbsp lemon juice
- 1 tsp brown sugar
- 2 tsp sesame oil
- 1 small fresh chilli, finely sliced or 1 Tbsp Thai hot chilli sauce

Sun-Dried Tomato Glaze
- 1 Tbsp sun-dried tomato pesto
- 1 large clove garlic, finely grated
- 1 Tbsp balsamic or wine vinegar
- ½ tsp crumbled dried oreganum
- 1 Tbsp olive oil

When you want shorter barbecue cooking time or want to make sure your barbecued chicken is cooked right to the bone, precook whole chicken legs two at a time in the microwave. Dry the legs on paper towels, brush them with enough soy sauce to coat them, then wrap in greaseproof or baking paper parcels, or place in oven bags. Microwave each pair of legs at 70% power for 7 minutes, turning once during cooking. (Chicken is cooked when juice from the thickest part runs clear, not pink, when pierced.) Precook remaining chicken in the same way.

Combine the glaze ingredients in screw-topped jars, shake well and refrigerate until needed. (Glazes will keep refrigerated for a week.) Brush unwrapped, precooked chicken legs with one of the glazes and barbecue for 8–10 minutes, turning to brown both sides. Brush with more glaze at intervals if desired.

VARIATION: For extra-fast grilled chicken, follow the same pre-cooking procedure.

hot tips for
grilled & barbecued chicken

Barbecued and grilled chicken is delicious, but not always trouble-free. To solve problems:

Chicken Cuts to Grill or Barbecue

Tenders. Small, lean, cook quickly, close to heat. Use marinade. Glaze near end of cooking time. Don't overcook.

Boneless, skinless breast. Very lean. Use marinade to keep moist. Cook further from heat since centre is thick. Cooks more quickly and evenly if beaten out first. Glaze at end of cooking time.

Boneless, skinless thighs. Snip underside to prevent curling during cooking. Juicier and moister than breast meat. Marinate. Cook quickly, close to heat.

Whole legs, thighs, drumsticks, skin-on, bone-in. Thick pieces of meat – use lower heat or cook further from heat. Slash meat to bone for more even cooking. Precook skin to prevent flare-ups. (See page 51.)

Whole chickens. Hard to cook evenly in a short time. Cut down centre back and open flat. Slash thick parts. Likely to drip fat if barbecued.

Precook larger pieces of chicken before you grill or barbecue them, so you don't worry about uncooked areas near the bone.

Choose smaller, skinless boneless cuts which cook more quickly and evenly than bone-in cuts.

Skin (then marinate) larger cuts which are to be barbecued, to prevent unwanted flare-ups caused by fat in chicken skin.

Cooking time varies with the heat and distance of the chicken from it. Cook small boneless pieces with higher heat, close to heat source. For larger pieces, lower heat or move chicken further from heat. Chicken is cooked when juices run clear, not pink, when pierced in thickest part.

Marinades add flavour to chicken before it is cooked. Brush on extra marinade during cooking. Marinades often contain oil to keep the surface moist and prevent burning during cooking. See Satay Marinade, page 31; Thai Marinade, page 42; Two Minute Marinade, page 47. For Sweet Chilli Marinade, stir together 1 Tbsp each oil, light soy sauce and Thai sweet chilli sauce. For Greek Marinade, stir together ¼ cup olive oil, 1 tsp each paprika, minced garlic and oreganum, and 2 Tbsp lemon juice.

Glazes are brushed on to nearly-cooked meat. They usually contain sugar (juice, jam, sauces etc) so the surface browns attractively just before it is cooked. See Mustardy Citrus Glaze, Hot Sesame Glaze, Sun-Dried Tomato Glaze, all on page 52. For Apricot Glaze, mix together 2 Tbsp apricot jam, 2 tsp Dijon smooth mustard, 1 Tbsp each orange juice, olive (or other) oil and light soy sauce and ½ tsp minced garlic. For Traditional BBQ Glaze, stir together 2 Tbsp each tomato sauce and oil, 1 Tbsp each lemon juice and Worcestershire sauce and 1 tsp each paprika and garlic salt.

chicken & crispy-noodle salad

This tasty and interesting salad has a low-fat dressing, and makes a great lunch or dinner throughout the warmer months. Although it must be assembled at the last minute, the ingredients are prepared (and bought) ahead.

FOR 2 SERVINGS:

- 2 boneless, skinless chicken breasts
- 1 tsp sesame oil
- 1 tsp Kikkoman soy sauce
- 2–3 cups crisp lettuce, coarsely chopped
- salad vegetables
- about ¼ cup dressing (see below)
- 70–100g crispy noodles
- 1 Tbsp toasted sesame seeds or 2 Tbsp chopped roasted peanuts

DRESSING:

- 2 cloves garlic
- 1cm piece of fresh root ginger
- 1 small dried chilli pepper
- ¼ cup wine vinegar or rice vinegar
- ¼ cup Kikkoman soy sauce
- 2 Tbsp sugar
- 1 Tbsp sesame oil
- 1 Tbsp cornflour
- ½ cup water

Pound the chicken breasts between plastic until 1 cm thick, then coat with sesame oil and soy sauce and grill or pan-grill. Cook until the thickest part of the breast has turned milky white but do not overcook. (Cut to check this.)

Cut the crisp lettuce into strips about 1 cm wide and 6 cm long. Place in a bowl with two or three other salad vegetables **such as spring onion, coriander leaves, celery, cucumber, red pepper, sprouts**, cut into pieces of similar size where necessary.

To assemble, slice warm chicken breasts into diagonal strips 1 cm thick, and toss in about 2 Tbsp dressing.

Toss the salad mixture gently with about 2 Tbsp dressing.

Just before serving, pile up two layers of salad and noodles on each flat plate or salad bowl, and top with chicken.

NOTE: If salad is made ahead, the noodles will lose their crispness.

Sprinkle with sesame seeds or peanuts.

To make the dressing, roughly chop the garlic and ginger into a food processor or blender. Process with all remaining dressing ingredients except water until very finely chopped, then add the water, process briefly, and tip into a pot or pan.

Bring to the boil, stirring constantly, then pour into a lidded container and cool.

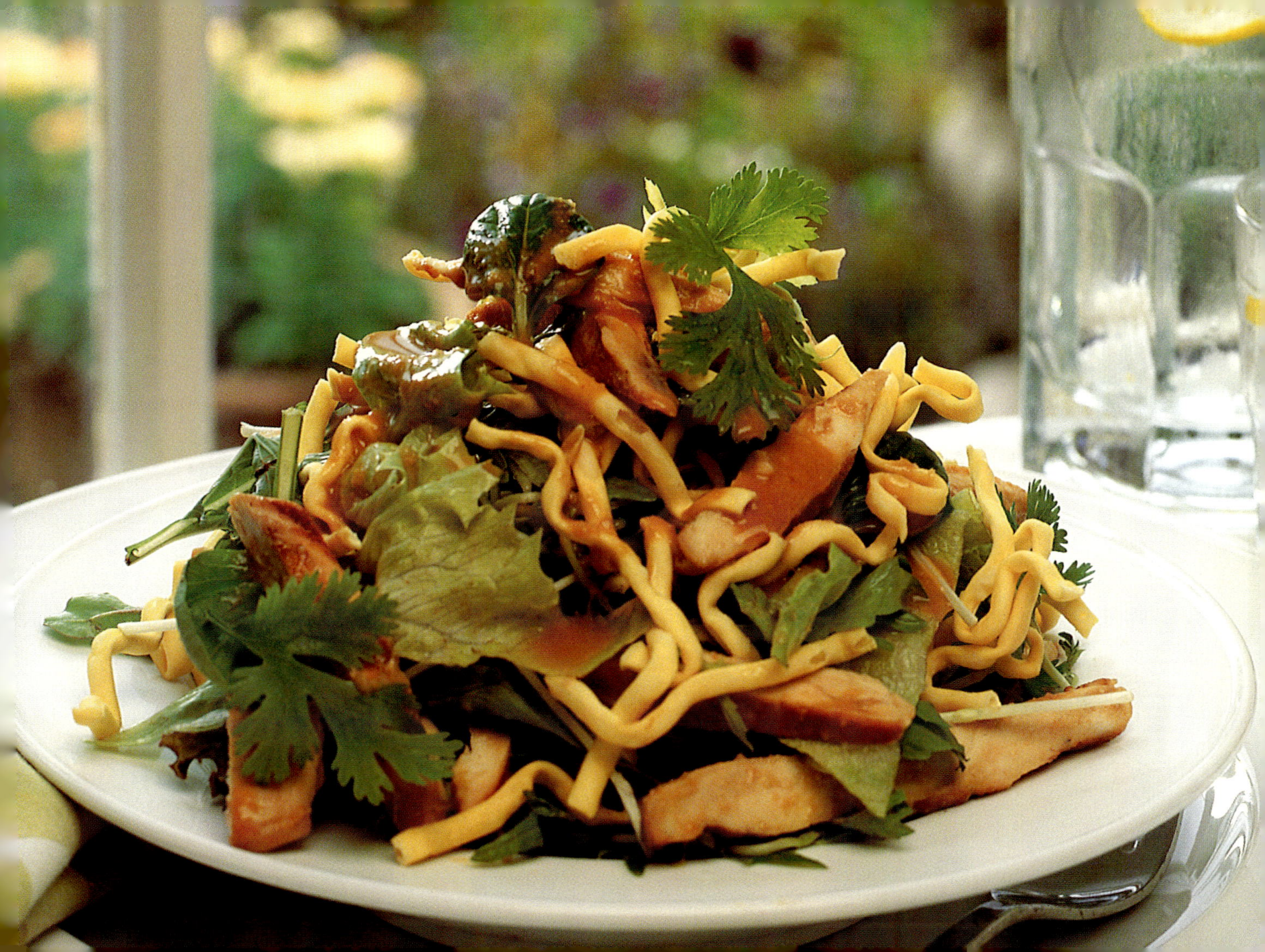

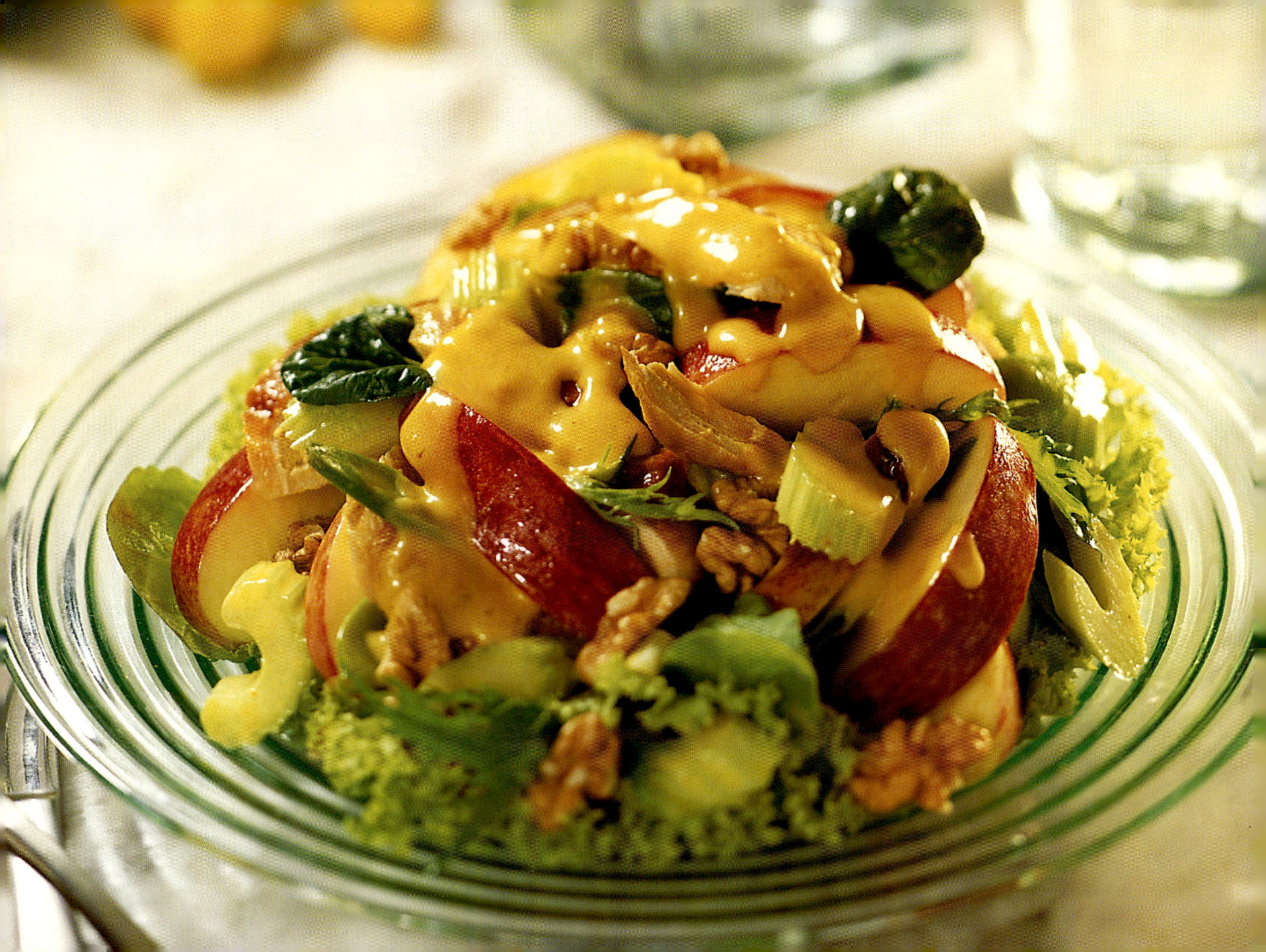

curried chicken salads

Chicken coated with curry-flavoured mayonnaise has long been an American favourite, but we find that creamy dressings based on sour cream are easier to make and are even nicer.

EACH FOR 2-4 SERVINGS:

Curried Sour Cream-Mustard Dressing
- 1 Tbsp sugar
- ¾ tsp salt
- 1 tsp curry powder or paste
- 1½ tsp smooth Dijon mustard
- 2 Tbsp each lemon juice, sour cream and canola oil

Curried Sour Cream & Mango Dressing
- ¼ cup sour cream
- 1–1½ tsp curry powder or paste
- 2 Tbsp chopped mango chutney
- ½ tsp salt
- 2–3 Tbsp chicken stock or water

To prepare either dressing, combine all ingredients in bowl then whisk until smooth. Put aside half dressing and thin the rest with water or chicken stock to coating consistency.

For either salad use sliced or diced flesh from the breast or leg of moist grilled, baked or roast chicken, bought pre-cooked chicken or smoked chicken. Using a sharp knife, slice it attractively, or cut in 1cm cubes. If not using immediately, cover and refrigerate. Wash salad greens and any fresh herbs you like, break into suitable pieces, roll up in a paper towel (as you would roll a sponge roll), then refrigerate until needed.

For Curried Chicken Waldorf Salad: Cut 1–1½ crisp unpeeled red apples into wedges or cubes, then sprinkle with lemon juice, cover and refrigerate. (Don't do this more than 30 minutes before serving, or apple may brown.) Cut the celery into 5mm thick slices cut into small cubes, then add to a large bowl with 150g–200g sliced or cubed cooked boneless chicken (as above), about ¼ cup best quality shelled walnuts and a selection of salad herbs and greens. Add the thinned portion of Curried Sour Cream-Mustard Dressing and toss together. Arrange salad on individual plates and serve with the extra dressing for diners to add as desired.

For Curried Chicken and Kumara Salad: Scrub and cut the ends off 2 small golden fleshed kumara (about 200g each) then wrap in cling-film and microwave. (Kumara is cooked when it gives when pressed, probably between 5 and 6 minutes.) Cool, peel off skin and slice. Toss cooked kumara with 150g–200g cooked boneless chicken (as above), ¼ cup chopped roasted peanuts or cashews, a handful of salad herbs and/or greens and the thinned Curried Sour Cream & Mango Dressing. Arrange salad on individual plates and serve with the extra dressing for diners to add as desired.

PICTURE OPPOSITE: CURRIED CHICKEN WALDORF SALAD

chicken caesar salad

This salad makes a great main course in hot weather. Although it takes some time and effort to get everything ready, it is really a complete meal containing chicken, vegetables and bread in the one bowl. Prepare it ahead, then assemble it in a short time when you want a meal in a hurry.

FOR 2 SERVINGS:

- croutons, bought or home-made
- 2–4 Tbsp dressing (see below)
- ½ small iceberg lettuce or 1 small cos (Romaine) lettuce
- 200–300g smoked chicken, sliced (or freshly grilled chicken breast meat)
- 6–8 pieces sun-dried tomatoes, (optional)
- freshly grated Parmesan cheese

Dressing
- 2–3 cloves garlic
- 1 small can anchovy fillets
- 2 Tbsp capers
- 2 halves sun-dried tomatoes (optional)
- 1 Tbsp Dijon style mustard
- 2 tsp sugar
- 1 cup olive oil
- 2 Tbsp wine vinegar
- 2 Tbsp Balsamic vinegar or extra wine vinegar
- 2 tsp minced chilli (optional)

Croutons: To make the croutons, cut one bread roll (or the same length of French bread) into thin slices with a sharp knife. Mix together 2 Tbsp olive oil, 2 Tbsp grated Parmesan cheese and 1 crushed clove of garlic, and brush the mixture on one side of each slice. Place, brushed side up, on an oven tray sprayed with non-stick spray or lined with a Teflon liner. Bake at 200°C for 5–7 minutes, or until lightly browned and crisp. Use immediately or put aside in an airtight container for a few days, warming before use.

Dressing: This delicious dressing is similar to a traditional Caesar Salad dressing, but does not contain egg. Combine all ingredients in a food processor bowl. If you like the definite, strong, savoury (but not fishy) taste of anchovies, use the oil as well. Otherwise drain off and discard it. Do not add any salt because the anchovies provide the salt needed in the dressing. Process all ingredients together until smooth, then transfer to a screw-topped jar. Use immediately or store in the refrigerator for up to 2 weeks, warming before use, as olive oil sets when refrigerated.

To make salad: For best results, prepare and refrigerate the crisp lettuce leaves several hours before the salad is to be eaten. Spread the washed leaves on a length of paper towel, then roll up like a sponge roll and refrigerate. (The leaves will stay cold, dry and crisp for hours.)

To serve, place the lettuce leaves on two plates, then arrange between them chunky slices of smoked chicken, strips of sun-dried tomatoes and croutons. Just before eating, drizzle 1–2 tablespoons of dressing over each salad. (Serve extra dressing, and the Parmesan cheese, so diners can help themselves if they like.)

NOTE: This salad has "un-caesar" additions. Leave out the sun-dried tomato if this worries you, and add an egg yolk to the dressing!

peanutty chicken salad

This is a good mixture to make the day after you have cooked a large chicken. (Or start with half a rotisseried chicken or a smoked chicken breast.) The dressed chicken and vegetable combination is very versatile. Enjoy it in different ways.

FOR 4 SERVINGS:

- 2 cups cooked chicken, bones removed, cut in bite-sized pieces
- 2 spring onions, sliced diagonally
- 2–4 cups crisp, coarsely shredded lettuce
- about 2 cups prepared crisp vegetables
- 1 cup roasted peanuts, chopped, or toasted sesame seeds
- dressing as required

Easy Peanut Dressing:
- ¼ cup crunchy peanut butter
- ½–1 tsp minced chilli
- 1 tsp sesame oil
- 2 Tbsp light soy sauce
- ½–1 tsp finely chopped garlic
- ½ tsp salt
- 2 Tbsp sugar
- 2 Tbsp wine vinegar
- ¼–½ cup water

To make the salad, vary the suggested quantities to suit yourself. Refrigerate the prepared chicken and spring onions together in a plastic bag. Prepare the lettuce and other salad ingredients such as **bean sprouts, thin strips of celery, red pepper, carrots, green beans, and snow peas** and place them in another plastic bag. Refrigerate until serving time.

When required, toss together the chicken, vegetables and half the peanuts and sesame seeds, then moisten the mixture with as much of the dressing as you like. Sprinkle each serving with the rest of the peanuts or sesame seeds.

To make the dressing, mix in a bowl or combine in a food processor all the dressing ingredients except the water, then add lukewarm water until dressing is the consistency of cream. Adjust seasonings to taste and store in an airtight jar. Keep unused dressing in the refrigerator, warming to room temperature before using, and thinning down with more water if it thickens. Always check flavour before using, since it may need balancing after standing.

Serve the salad in any of the following ways:

- packed into toasted, split pita breads, or piled in split rolls or French bread
- rolled up in mountain or naan bread
- piled on extra shredded lettuce, alone, or layered with deep-fried rice noodles or bought crispy noodles
- with or without the lettuce, folded gently through room-temperature cooked noodles or other pasta moistened with the same dressing.

optional extras
for roast chicken

Gravy and stuffing turn a plainly roasted chicken into something special and also make it go further!

Gravy

Gravy is made from the drippings left in a roasting pan after the cooked chicken has been taken out of it.

Tilt the roasting pan so the drippings run into one corner. Pour or spoon off (and discard) any extra chicken fat, leaving 2–3 Tbsp of fat and some brownish drippings. Pour these into a non-stick frypan and mix in 3 Tbsp flour. Stir over moderate heat, until the mixture bubbles and darkens, then stir in 1½ cups of vegetable cooking liquid, chicken stock or water.

Simmer, stirring all the time, for about 5 minutes, until mixture thickens. If it is pale, add a teaspoon of soy sauce. Taste and add salt and pepper if necessary. Pour (or strain if lumpy) into a jug or bowl, and serve with the sliced chicken.

Stuffing

Stuffing may be cooked inside a chicken while it roasts. However, if you put the unstuffed chicken on to cook, then make the stuffing and cook it separately, you will save time and the chicken will cook more evenly.

- 1 onion, chopped
- 1 stalk celery, chopped finely, optional
- ¼ tsp each thyme, sage, oreganum (or other herbs)
- 2 tsp butter
- about 100g stale bread, crumbed (to make 2–3 cups breadcrumbs)
- 1 egg
- ½ tsp salt
- ¼ cup currants or Californian raisins (optional)
- ¼–½ cup chopped dried apricots (optional)
- ¼ cup pinenuts or chopped almonds (optional)

Cook the onion, celery if using, and herbs in the butter in a covered pot or pan over low heat for 5–10 minutes, until onion is tender but not browned.

Crumb the bread in a food processor and add the egg (or break the bread into pieces, put it in a bowl with the egg, and leave it to soften for a few minutes, then mash with a fork). To either mixture, stir in the salt, onion mixture, dried fruit and nuts.

Butter a square of foil, form a roll of stuffing on it, and fold the foil to enclose it. Bake stuffing alongside the chicken for 30–40 minutes until it is firm.

VARIATION: Replace breadcrumbs with cooked rice, burghul or couscous if desired.

home-made chicken
stock

Home-made chicken stock gives body and extra flavour to many chicken dishes. Freeze the following stocks in small tubs or pottles (eg cottage cheese pottles).

Stock from Raw Chicken

Freeze raw chicken necks and trimmings in a heavy weight plastic bag, adding to the bag until it is full. Use alone, or with fresh chicken backs for stock.

FOR 8 CUPS:

- about 1kg of raw chicken bones, chicken backs, skin, giblets, feet etc.
- 12 cups (3 litres) water
- 1 tsp finely chopped garlic
- 1 onion, chopped roughly
- 2–3 bay leaves, if available
- about 12 peppercorns
- ½–1 tsp each dried oreganum and thyme
- 1 tsp salt

Simmer everything in a large covered pot, for 3 hours. Sieve and discard the solids. Skim off and discard the fat from the surface. Refrigerate or freeze as above.

Stock from Cooked Chicken Bones

The bones from roast, barbecued, grilled or baked chicken make useful, small amounts of good stock. Start the stock cooking while you do the dishes!

FOR 2-4 CUPS:

- cooked carcass, chicken bones, giblets, skin, fat, etc.
- vegetable trimmings, if available
- 3-5 cups water (or saved vegetable cooking liquid) to cover
- ½ tsp salt, if not using vegetable cooking liquid
- 1–2 cloves garlic
- 1 carrot, onion and celery stalk, chopped roughly
- 1 Tbsp light soy sauce
- 6 peppercorns and/or 1 dried chilli

Put everything in a large pot, cover and simmer for 2 hours. Strain, discarding solids. Refrigerate or freeze.

Chicken Giblet Stock

Giblets make strongly flavoured stock with minimum cost, mess and effort.

FOR 6-7 CUPS:

- 500g chicken giblets
- 8 cups (2 litres) water
- 1–2 cloves garlic
- 1–2 slices fresh ginger, optional
- 1 Tbsp each light soy sauce and sherry
- 6 peppercorns or 1 dried chilli

Put everything in a large pot, cover and simmer for 3 hours. Strain, discarding giblets. Refrigerate or freeze.

index

Apricot Glaze	53
Baked Chicken & Rice	24
Ballti Chicken Curry	39
Barbecued Red Chicken	51
barbecued, hot tips for	53
barbecued, shortcut chicken legs	52
Billy's Special Chicken & Kumara Curry	45
bones, stock from	61
breasts & thighs, boneless, 5-spice chicken and	23
breasts & thighs, boneless, balti curry	39
breasts & thighs, boneless, butter chicken	41
breasts & thighs, boneless, Mexican	32
breasts & thighs, boneless, paprikash	20
breasts & thighs, boneless, stir-fried	17
breasts & thighs, boneless, wraps	14
breasts, barbecue and grilling tips	53
breasts, chicken & crispy noodle salad	54
breasts, chicken caesar salad	58
breasts, Florentine	29
breasts, Pat's Cuban	30
breasts, satay sticks	31
breasts, Thai-flavoured stir-fried	42
Burritos, chicken	13, 14
butter chicken, Simon's	41
Caesar salad, chicken	58
casserole, country captain	34
casserole, curried pineapple	19
casserole, fruity chicken	19
casserole, Moroccan chicken	36
casserole, packet soups	19
casserole, sherried chicken with mushrooms	19
Cheats "Roast" Chicken	12
Chicken & Crispy Noodle Salad	54
chicken and tomatoes, spiced	18
Chicken & Vegetable Curry	35
Chicken Baked on Rice One Pan Dinner	24
Chicken Breasts Florentine	29
Chicken Caesar Salad	58
Chicken Giblet Stock	61
Chicken Paprikash	20
Chicken Wraps	14
chicken, precooked	13
cooked chicken, peanutty chicken salad	59
cooked chicken, wraps, rolls, quesadillas	14
Country Captain Chicken	34
Creamy Chicken on Pasta	13
crispy noodle, chicken and	54
Croutons	58
Cuban chicken, Pat's	30
Curried Chicken and Kumara Salad	57
Curried Chicken Salads	57
Curried Chicken Waldorf Salad	57
Curried Pineapple Chicken	19
curry, balti	39
curry, chicken and vegetable	35
Dressing, chicken & crispy noodle salad	54
dressing, chicken caesar salad	58
dressing, easy peanut	59
dressing, sesame	40
Easy Oriental Simmered Chicken	40
Easy Peanut Dressing	59
Easy Salsa Fresca	29
Five-Spice Chicken with Fresh Noodles	23
flat breads, chicken under wraps	14
Florentine, chicken breasts	29
fresh noodles, five-spice chicken with	23
Fruity Chicken Casserole	19
Giblets, stock from	61
glaze, apricot	53
glaze, hot sesame	52
glaze, mustardy citrus	52
glaze, sun-dried tomato	52
glaze, traditional barbecue	53
glazes	53
Grandma's Whole Chicken Pot Roast	25
Gravy	60
Greek Marinade	53
grilled breast, chicken caesar salad	58
grilled, hot tips for	53
grilled, shortcut chicken legs	52
Home-made Chicken Stock	61
Hot Sesame Glaze	52
Hot Tips for Grilled & Barbecued Chicken	53
Kiwifruit Salsa	30
Legs, 30 minute roast with vegetables	11
legs, barbecue and grilling tips	53
legs, barbecued red	51
legs, barbecued shortcut	52
legs, lemon roast	11
lemon roast chicken	8
lemon roast legs	11
Making stock	61
Mango Salsa	30
marinade, Greek	53
marinade, sweet chilli	53
marinades	53
Mexican Chicken	32
Mexican seasoning	32
microwaved rice	17
Microwaved "Roast" Chicken	7
microwaved "Roast" pieces	7
Moroccan Chicken	36
mushrooms, sherried chicken casserole	19
Mustardy Citrus Glaze	52
Nibbles, see pieces	

noodle salad, chicken and	54	rice, and baked chicken dinner	24	Stir-Fried Chicken	17
noodles, five-spice chicken with fresh	23	rice, microwaved	17	stir-fried chicken, Thai-flavoured	42
One-pan dinner, 30 minute	26	roast chicken dinner, cheats	12	Stock from Cooked Chicken	61
Optional Extras for Roast Chicken	60	roast chicken, 30 minute with vegetables	11	Stock from Raw Chicken	61
Paprika Drumsticks with Pan-Baked Scones	48	roast chicken, gravy for	60	stock, chicken giblet	61
paprikash, chicken	20	roast chicken, microwaved	7	stocks, home-made chicken	61
pasta, chicken paprikash	20	roast chicken, plain	6	Stuffing	60
pasta, creamy chicken on	13	roast chicken, stuffing for	60	Sun-Dried Tomato Glaze	52
Pat's Cuban Chicken	30	roast chicken, wine glazed	6	Sweet Chilli Marinade	53
peanut sauce, quick	31	Roast Lemon Chicken	8	**T**acos	13
Peanutty Chicken Salad	59	**S**alad rolls	14	tenders, barbecue and grilling tips	53
pieces, 30 minute dinner	26	salad, chicken & crispy noodle	54	tenders, see boneless breasts & thighs	
pieces, baked chicken and rice dinner	24	salad, chicken and kumara	57	Teriyaki Chicken	33
pieces, barbecue and grilling tips	53	salad, chicken caesar	58	Thai-flavoured Stir-Fried Chicken	42
pieces, barbecued red	51	salad, curried chicken Waldorf	57	Thai Green Chicken Curry	46
pieces, barbecued shortcut	52	salad, peanutty chicken	59	thighs, barbecue and grilling tips	53
pieces, chicken and mushroom casserole	19	salads, curried chicken	57	thighs, see breasts & thighs, boneless	
pieces, chicken and vegetable curry	35	salsa fresca	29	Thirty-Minute Chicken Dinner	26
pieces, country captain casserole	34	salsa, kiwifruit	30	Thirty-Minute Roast Chicken and Vegetables	11
pieces, curried pineapple casserole	19	salsa, mango	30	tomatoes, spiced chicken and	18
pieces, easy oriental simmered	40	satay sticks	31	Tortillas, chicken	13, 14
pieces, fruity chicken casserole	19	sauce, satay	31	Traditional Barbecue Glaze	53
pieces, microwaved roast	7	seasoning, Mexican	32	Two-Minute Chicken Breasts	47
pieces, Moroccan chicken	36	sesame dressing	40	**W**hole, cheats roast	12
pieces, sesame-soy	33	sesame-soy pieces	33	whole chicken, barbecue and grilling tips	53
pieces, souped-up casseroles	19	Sherried Chicken with Mushrooms	19	whole, Grandma's pot roast	25
pieces, spiced with tomatoes	18	Shortcut Barbecued or Grilled Chicken Legs	52	whole microwaved roast	7
pieces, Teriyaki	33	simmered chicken, easy oriental	40	whole roast lemon	6
pineapple, curried chicken casserole	19	Simon's Butter Chicken	41	whole roast wine glazed	6
plain roast chicken	6	smoked chicken, chicken caesar salad	58	Wine Glazed Roast Chicken	6
pot roast, Grandma's whole	25	Souped-Up Chicken Casseroles	19	wings, see pieces	
precooked chicken, starting with	13	spiced chicken and pasta	18	wraps, chicken and rice	14
Quesadillas, chicken	14	Spiced Chicken and Tomatoes	18	wraps, chicken under	14
Quick Chicken Satay Sticks	31	spiced chicken on rice	18	wraps, easy oriental simmered chicken	14
quick satay sauce	31	spiced chicken with beans	18	wraps, Moroccan chicken	14
Red chicken, barbecued	51	Start with a Pre-cooked Chicken	13	wraps, Simon's butter chicken	14

Knives
by Mail Order

For about 20 years I have imported my favourite, very sharp, kitchen knives from Switzerland. They keep their edges well, are easy to sharpen, a pleasure to use, and make excellent gifts.

VEGETABLE KNIFE $8.00
Ideal for cutting and peeling vegetables, these knives have a straight edged 85mm blade and black (dishwasher-proof) nylon handle. Each knife comes in an individual plastic sheath.

BONING/UTILITY KNIFE $9.50
Excellent for boning chicken and other meats, and/or general kitchen duties. Featuring a 103mm blade that curves to a point and a dishwasher-proof, black nylon handle, each knife comes in a plastic sheath.

SERRATED KNIFE $9.50
I find these knives unbelievably useful and I'm sure you will too! They are perfect for cutting cooked meats, ripe fruit and vegetables, and slicing bread and baking. Treated carefully, these blades stay sharp for years. The serrated 110mm blade is rounded at the end with a black (dishwasher-proof) nylon handle. Each knife comes in an individual plastic sheath.

THREE-PIECE SET $20.00
This three-piece set includes a vegetable knife, a serrated knife (as described above) and a right-handed potato peeler with a matching black handle, presented in a white plastic wallet.

GIFT BOXED KNIFE SET $44.00
This set contains five knives plus a matching right-handed potato peeler. There is a straight bladed vegetable knife and a serrated knife (as above), as well as a handy 85mm serrated blade vegetable knife, a small (85mm) utility knife with a pointed tip and a smaller (85mm) serrated knife. These elegantly presented sets make ideal gifts.

SERRATED CARVING KNIFE $28.50
This fabulous knife cuts beautifully and is a pleasure to use. The 21cm serrated blade does not require sharpening. Once again the knife has a black moulded, dishwasher safe handle and comes in a plastic sheath.

STEEL $20.00
The steel has 20cm blade and measures 33cm in total. With its matching black handle the steel is an ideal companion to your own knives, or as a gift. I have had excellent results using the steel. N.B. Not for use with serrated knives.

PROBUS SPREADER/SCRAPER $5.50
After my knives, these are the most used tool in my kitchen! With a comfortable plastic handle, metal shank and flexible plastic blade (suitable for use on non-stick surfaces), these are excellent for mixing muffin batters, stirring and scraping bowls, spreading icings, turning pikelets etc.

NON-STICK TEFLON LINERS
I regard these SureBrand Teflon liners as another essential kitchen item. They really help avoid the frustration of stuck-on baking, roasting or frying. Once you've used them, you'll wonder how you did without!

Round tin liner (for 15-23cm tins)	$5.50
Round tin liner (for 23-30cm tins)	$8.50
Square tin liner (for 15-23cm tins)	$5.50
Square tin liner (for 23-30cm tins)	$8.50
Ring tin liner (for 23cm tins)	$5.95
Baking sheet liner (33x44cm)	$10.95

Prices as at 1 March 1999, all prices include GST. **Please add $3.50 post & packing to any knife/spreader order (any number of items). Please note, Teflon prices <u>include</u> post & packing.**

Make cheques payable to Alison Holst Mail Orders and post to: Alison Holst Mail Orders
Freepost 124807
PO Box 17016
Wellington